# The Sermon without End

# Praise for *The Sermon without End*

"*The Sermon without End* develops a comprehensive, generous, and readable argument for a less assertive-argumentative and more conversational approach to preaching. Without accommodating or overreacting to postmodern culture, Allen and Allen invite preachers to rethink sermons as genuine conversations about the meaning of the gospel with the many and diverse persons in their increasingly multicultural and multireligious 'neighborhoods.' This book reads like a breath of fresh air in the midst of the often-stifling debate about what churches need to be doing in postmodern culture."
—John S. McClure, Charles G. Finney Professor of Preaching and Worship, Vanderbilt Divinity School, Nashville, TN

"I encourage you to join Ron Allen and Wes Allen's walking tour. They will help you see the neighborhoods and dwellings preachers and congregations inhabit in new eye-opening ways. These habitations have nurtured and encouraged but, as the authors suggest, they are not where we should be living in this postmodern age of rapidly changing cultures. Allen and Allen invite us to move to a new neighborhood of postapologetic preaching. This neighborhood is one shaped by listening, respecting the other, and reciprocating conversations that contribute to the way our preaching helps to make meaning in God's world."
—Lucy Lind Hogan, Hugh Latimer Elderdice Professor of Preaching and Worship, Wesley Theological Seminary, Washington, DC

"Allen and Allen present a conversational approach to theology and preaching that takes seriously the church's location between modernity and postmodernity. Their lively and accessible imagery will encourage preachers to take a closer look at their own 'homiletic neighborhoods' as they search for words to engage in reciprocal, unending conversations with a multitude of others."
—Sarah Travis, Sessional Lecturer and Minister in Residence, Knox College, Toronto School of Theology, Toronto, ON

"This is an important, timely book. Ron Allen and Wesley Allen invite us into a powerful new way of practicing preaching as a conversation. For them conversation is not just one more preaching style—not even just a method. For Allen and Allen, preaching as conversation is a way of doing theology that opens up preaching more profoundly to others. If you sense that real depth is missing in preaching today, be sure to read *The Sermon without End*."
—David Schnasa Jacobsen, Professor of the Practice of Homiletics and Director of the Homiletical Theology Project, Boston University School of Theology, Boston, MA

# The Sermon without End

## A Conversational Approach to Preaching

Ronald J. Allen
O. Wesley Allen, Jr.

Abingdon Press

*Nashville*

THE SERMON WITHOUT END:
A CONVERSATIONAL APPROACH TO PREACHING

*Copyright © 2015 by Abingdon Press*

*This book is printed on acid-free paper.*

**Library of Congress Cataloging-in-Publication Data has been requested.**

15 16 17 18 19 20 21 22 23 24—10 9 8 7 6 5 4 3 2 1
MANUFACTURED IN THE UNITED STATES OF AMERICA

*For our faculty colleagues
at Christian Theological Seminary
and Lexington Theological Seminary—
thank you for being conversation partners
who have led us deeper into Christian faith across the years.*

# Table of Contents

# Introduction

Stanley Hauerwas and William H. Willimon open their influential book, *Resident Aliens*, with a wonderful story.

> Sometime between 1960 and 1980, an old, inadequately conceived world ended, and a fresh, new world began. . . .
>
> When and how did we change? Although it may sound trivial, one of us [Willimon] is tempted to date the shift sometime on a Sunday evening in 1963. Then, in Greenville, South Carolina, in defiance of the state's time-honored blue laws, the Fox Theater opened on Sunday. Seven of us—regular attenders of the Methodist Youth Fellowship at Buncombe Street Church—made a pact to enter the front door of the church, be seen, then quietly slip out the back door and join John Wayne at the Fox.
>
> That evening has come to represent a watershed in the history of Christendom, South Carolina style. On that night, Greenville, South Carolina—the last pocket of resistance to secularity in the Western world—served notice that it would no longer be a prop for the church. There would be no more free passes for the church, no more free rides. The Fox Theater went head to head with the church over who would provide the world view for the young. That night in 1963, the Fox Theater won the opening skirmish.[1]

Hauerwas and Willimon draw the conclusion that the mid-twentieth century fall of Christendom (or the façade of Christendom) signals

---

1. Stanley Hauerwas and William H. Willimon, *Resident Alien: Life in the Christian Colony* (Nashville: Abingdon Press, 1989), 15–16.

that the church is and should be in exile from the wider culture. The church (following the likes of Rudolf Bultmann and Paul Tillich), they say, slides down the slippery slope of unfaithfulness to the countercultural gospel when it engages in apologetics; that is, when it asks, "How do we make the gospel credible to the modern world?" In contrast, they follow Karl Barth in rejecting apologetics, view the church as a culture unto itself properly standing over against secular culture instead of engaging it, and argue that the proper question for theology is, "How do we make the world credible to the gospel?"[2]

The story is provocative and insightful but not without problems. One problem with the story (and with taking a lesson from it about the way the church is to approach sharing its faith in the twenty-first century) is simply that is no longer 1963.[3] If we return to Greenville, South Carolina, today and go looking for the Fox Theater, we would not find it. It closed in 1978. It has been replaced by various multiplexes around the city showing films from around the world at all times of the day. The day is long past when everyone who wants to go to a movie (on Sunday evening) is forced to watch and buy into the essence of American, white masculinity represented by John Wayne. We can find choices to fit nearly every interest, taste, existential investment, and worldview.

In any given theater in Greenville, we can walk into the movie of our choice with members of the millenial, generation X, baby boomer, silent, and greatest generations carrying our foods of choice—popcorn and Coke, nachos and Icees, hotdogs and iced tea, or ice cream Dippin' Dots. The seats around us might be filled with people of Native American, European, African, Caribbean, Central American, Latin American, Middle Eastern, and Asian descent. We might find people who are men, women, gay, straight, bisexual, transsexual, and transgender. We might

---

2. Ibid., 15–24.

3. For a variety of responses to *Resident Aliens* twenty-five years after it was published, see "State of the Colony: *Resident Aliens* at 25," *Christian Century* 131, no. 20 (October 1, 2014): 22–34.

see single people, couples, groups of friends, and families. We might have a social conservative sitting to our left and a liberal to our right. We could notice people from a cross section of socioeconomic statuses. We might find Christians, Muslims, Hindus, Buddhists, Jews along with those whose are spiritual-but-not-religious, agnostic, and atheist—and some of them carpooled together. And until the movie begins, we would almost certainly see people from all these different cultural divisions and cross divisions looking at their smart phones, checking e-mail, texting, surfing ranges of sites from the Internet. Toto, we're not in the twentieth century anymore.

Hauerwas and Willimon were partly correct in their analysis of that Sunday evening at the Fox Theater in 1963 when Willimon snuck away from church to watch a movie. That night did represent the end of Christendom. But that really is because it represented the end of modernity. It was the beginning of the end of homogeneity in our society (that is, the end of the façade of homogeneity as perceived by many people of European origin). From our point of view, the church today exists in, and must speak to and with, an ever-increasingly pluralistic and globalized culture.

The dynamics of diversity, or the culture of otherness represented in the multiplex, however, is not only a phenomenon of the secular society in which the church exists. We cannot say, "The church is in pluralism but not of it." If we walk into morning worship in many churches, we will find the same dynamic of a cross-cultural gathering that we observed in the theater, even if it is not to the same degree of diversity. Radically different understandings of God, self, neighbor, and world bounce this way and that off the walls of the sanctuary in a manner analogous to the sounds of banjos, djembes, cellos, electric guitars, and, yes, pianos and pipe organs meshing and clashing with lyrics in English, Spanish, and Swahili in a global music mash-up.

Any approach to the Christian faith that assumes the church can isolate itself from the multilingual interaction and multivalent interpretation that is constant in the twenty-first century is anachronistic and naïve. For the church and its preaching to be relevant in this new and constantly shifting age, a new way forward is needed.

Historically, the church has used the rubric of apologetics to describe how the church engages the culture in which it resides and participates. A traditional definition of apologetics is as follows:

> *A theological/homiletical approach that uses the categories of knowledge, thinking, and values of the contemporary culture to explain and defend the faith in response to explicit or implicit misunderstanding, challenges, and attacks in order to commend that very faith.*[4]

In chapter 1 we will explore this definition and examine the three broad approaches to apologetics that have dominated modernity. We will use metaphors drawn from ways of living with one's neighbors to classify these approaches. The first is the Hatfields and McCoys approach to apologetics—a feud between faith and reason, between the church and culture. In this approach the church apologetically defends the faith against assertions in society that conflict with scripture because scripture cannot be wrong . . . because the God who inspired it cannot be wrong. The second approach is characterized by an apartment building in which faith, the tenant, pays rent to reason, the landlord. The church apologetically accommodates its theology and proclamation to the reasonable assertion of culture. The third approach is that of a gated community in which the church and culture live in different neighborhoods. Faith and

---

4. This definition is informed by the variety of approaches to define apologetics found in the following reference works: Alan Richardson, "Apologetics, Apologists, Apology," in *A Dictionary of Christian Theology*, ed. Alan Richardson (Philadelphia: Westminster, 1969); James C. Livingston, "Apologetics," in *The Dictionary of Bible and Religion*, ed. William H. Gentz (Nashville: Abingdon Press, 1986), 59; Horst G. Pöhlmann, "Apologetics," in *The Encyclopedia of Christianity* (Grand Rapids: William B. Eerdmans, 1998), 1.102–5; William A. Dryness, "Apologetics," in *Global Dictionary of Theology*, ed. William A. Dyrness and Veli-Matti Kärkkäinen (Downers Grove: IVP Academic, 2008), 55–59.

reason may live near each other, but they speak different dialects. In this approach, the church rejects apologetics altogether.

Given these three approaches to apologetics in modernity, what approach is called for in *post*modernity? Should a pastor preach apologetically in the twenty-first century? We answer this question with a resounding yes and no. Yes, it is the preacher's job to explain and defend the faith in order to commend that faith to any who will hear the church's proclamation. And this must certainly be done in terms accessible to those who would listen (i.e., in language that engages contemporary knowledge, thinking, and values).

But, no, the traditional definition of apologetics operating in modernity implies forms of interaction between the church and the world that are not quite at home in the postmodern ethos. In traditional apologetics the terms of communication are defined by the culture but the communication itself is from the church to the culture. Paradoxically and unacceptably, this approach subordinates proclamation and interpretation of the Christian gospel to cultural forms of expression while placing culture in the subordinate position of passively receiving the gospel the church offers.

Thus in place of an apologetic approach to preaching, we propose a *post*apologetic homiletical approach—an approach that is conversational, seeking critical reciprocity between the many and varied voices in, around, and outside of the church. This approach is post-evangelical in that it moves beyond attempts to defend a premodern understanding of the faith over against evolving scientific and philosophical thought. It is postmodern in the sense that it moves beyond the liberal tradition of accommodating the gospel to evolving thought. And it is post-postliberal in that it recognizes and values that intercultural dialogue is ever present, causing the continued evolution of scientific, philosophical, and religious thought.

*Introduction*

In chapter 1 we review the evangelical, liberal, and postliberal neighborhoods in relation to modernist apologetics. In chapter 2 we propose a postapologetic stance we argue is appropriate for postmodernity. Chapter 3 offers a conversational homiletic that accords with this postapologetic stance. And chapter 4 offers practical advice for preparing a conversational sermon along with a case study of such a sermon.

# Apologetic Neighborhoods

I f we conducted a survey of contemporary preachers and congregations to measure the frequency of the use of the language of "apologetics," we would find that such language appears often in some neighborhoods of the church and not at all in others. For example, evangelicals tend to use the language of apologetics more than progressives. However, regardless of whether today's preacher or congregation regularly uses the language of apologetics, the concern at the heart of apologetics is a concern at the heart of Christian community in every generation: the search for real confidence in God, the Christian message, and the values and practices of Christian life, particularly in the face of challenges to that confidence. Such challenges may be direct, as when a group outside (or inside) the church claims that aspects of the church's beliefs and behavior are not tenable. Or they may be indirect, as when a dimension of a contemporary worldview seems to contradict something assumed in a prior era of history.

What can we truly believe in the way of theological claims and ethical perspectives? And what reasons give us the deep sense we can believe and act in those ways, especially when questions and uncertainties come into view? How do we answer critics from outside the church who charge that Christian faith is no longer believable? How do we respond to voices within the church (and sometimes within the preacher) that question our interpretation of Christian faith and practice and who may even challenge the validity of faith?

Preachers and theologians sometimes discuss such matters under the rubric of the relationship between faith and reason. To what degree is a congregation's faith reasonable, that is, believable in the sociohistorical period in which the congregation lives? To be sure, the specific issues of faith and reason change from period to period. Preachers and congregations deal with these matters in different ways according to the presuppositions and resources of their different moments in history. Yet while criteria for a faith in which a congregation can have confidence vary from theological neighborhood to theological neighborhood, the search for such a faith persists.

This chapter sketches the broad landscape over which we will set our homiletical proposal. We first offer a standard definition of apologetics and then look briefly at how different specific issues in apologetics surface in different seasons of the history of the church, even as the apologetic task extends from generation to generation. The heart of the chapter describes three of the main approaches to apologetics from the twentieth century that are still making claims on the church of the twenty-first century (evangelical, liberal, and postliberal). These approaches were developed to deal with various challenges to the faith posed by modernism.

# Defining Apologetics

To begin considering the question of the appropriateness of preaching being apologetic in character, we return to the traditional definition of apologetics offered in the introduction and examined here in detail:

*Apologetics is a theological/homiletical approach that uses the categories of knowledge, thinking, and values of the contemporary culture to explain and defend Christian faith in response to explicit or implicit misunderstanding, challenges, and attacks in order to commend that very faith.*

Apologetics, as defined here, commends the faith to two audiences simultaneously. At one level, an apology attempts to defend the faith to those *outside* the church by showing that Christian faith is credible. At another level, an apology reassures those *inside* the community that they can have confidence in their faith in a way that makes sense from the perspective of competing and compelling worldviews of their time. In this latter role, the apology does not seek so much to persuade or convert as to reinforce the trust of insiders in the ideas and practices of their faith.

The starting point of apologetics for both audiences is the *explicit or implicit misunderstanding of, challenges to, and attacks against* the Christian beliefs and practices. As one author puts it,

> In countering objections brought against Christian belief, apologetics does not itself determine the doctrines requiring defense. These are imposed by the criticisms, explicit or implicit, advanced by the unbeliever or critic. Therefore, because of fresh challenges brought by rival religions or by changes in secular knowledge, the apologetic task must be undertaken anew in every age.[1]

Apologetics assumes the church is in conversation (or debate) with the world. Voices from the world set the *beginning point* of the conversation (for both insider and outsider audiences) by raising issues that call into question aspects of the Christian faith and life. The apologist responds to those issues in ways that refute criticisms and offer reasons for believing that the apologist's vision of God, church, and world is convincing.

---

1. James C. Livingston, "Apologetics," in *The Dictionary of Bible and Religion*, ed. William H. Gentz (Nashville: Abingdon Press, 1986), 59.

Apologetics approaches misunderstandings, challenges, and attacks *using the categories of knowledge, thinking and values of the contemporary culture*. In other words, not only does the sociohistorical situation determine the scope of the conversation or debate between the church and that situation, the church uses the "language" of that situation not only to be understood but also in the hope that outsiders and insiders can and will accept Christian faith. Apologetics, therefore, is a "cultural theology" in the sense that the way it expresses interpretations of the Christian faith is dependent upon the worldview(s) it is addressing, even as an apology seeks to help its receivers interpret those worldviews theologically.

As the church's scriptures and traditions were not shaped in a vacuum without being culturally and historically conditioned, we cannot speak today, or any day, in a manner not shaped by the very day in which we speak. Theology is always and only spoken in a particular sociohistorical context to that particular context using the language of that particular context. Use of contemporary knowledge, thinking, and values in theology and preaching, then, is simply the fulfillment of the dictum that is a part of every introductory public speaking class: know your audience and craft your message in such a way that they can grasp it and be grasped by it.

Apologetics deals with contemporary challenges and draws on contemporary categories of thought to address them not as abstract theological ends unto themselves but specifically *to explain and defend the faith in order to commend that very faith*. Apologetics is not a self-serving exercise any more than the church is called to be a self-serving institution. As one author puts it, "Apologetic theology can be thought of as a specific theological method that interacts with the surrounding culture in the service of mission and evangelism. It is theology that seeks to express itself in contextual terms so that the gospel will be heard and understood."[2]

## *The Changing, Unchanging Apologetic Task*

As we noted above, the specific issues faced by apologetics change from generation to generation. The church continually focuses and refocuses its apologetic task according to the questions and challenges of its age. This book is not concerned directly with analyzing the history of the church's apologetic endeavors, but it is worth noting briefly that the apologetical approaches of modernity did not develop *ex nihilo*.[3]

Scholars generally agree that the earliest Christian apologetic practices in the first century CE are rooted in Judaism. Jewish writers explained their distinctive faith and practice to their own communities, as in many of the Torah, Prophets, and Writings. However, the Jewish apologetic task became more widespread and formal as Jewish people came into more and more contact with Greek culture in the wake of Alexander the Great (366–333 BCE) who brought much of the Mediterranean basin under Hellenistic influence. Some Gentile writers had caricatured Jews and made derogatory comments about Jewish ways of life (e.g., the dietary practices) and Jewish history. Jewish authors such as Josephus, Philo, and the author of the Letter to Aristeas shaped parts of their writings ostensibly to respond to outsider Gentile criticism while not only debunking such criticism for Jewish insiders but buttressing the confidence of Jewish readers in their own religion.

---

2. William A. Dryness, "Apologetics," in *Global Dictionary of Theology*, ed. William A. Dyrness and Veli-Matti Kärkkäinen (Downers Grove: IVP Academic, 2008), 55.

3. For fuller discussions of the history of apologetics than what is provided below, we suggest Avery Robert Dulles, *A History of Apologetics*, 2nd ed. (New York: Corpus, 1971); Kenneth D. Boa and Robert M. Bowman, Jr., *Faith Has Its Reasons: An Integrative Approach to Defending Christianity*, 2nd ed. (Waynesboro, GA: Paternoster, 2006), 1–32.

The New Testament does not include any writing that is primarily apologetic in nature. Biblical scholars do, however, recognize apologetic themes and scenes in various texts. Some of the more obvious types are

- narratives defending some claim of the church's faith (e.g., Jesus being declared innocent by Roman authorities in Matt 27:15-23 and Luke 23:4, 13-16; the guards at the tomb in Matt 27:62-66; 28:4, 11-15);

- models of preaching apologetically by drawing on contemporary philosophy (e.g., Paul's Areopagus speech in Acts 17);

- using natural theology to build a case for a Christian perspective (e.g., Rom 1:18–2:16); and

- instructions for giving a defense of the faith (e.g., Mark 13:11 par., Col 4:5-6; 1 Pet 3:15-16).

While these hints at apologetics in the New Testament show the authors' awareness of claims outside the church that must be countered, the New Testament documents were all written with an insider audience in mind. By making a defense concerning claims coming from outside the church, the authors give members of the community reason to remain steadfast in their own faith.

In the postbiblical period of early Christianity, the church's faith was misrepresented and attacked by some beyond the Christian community in more vigorous and sustained ways. A number of thinkers, called Apologists, emerged in the church in the second and third centuries to answer assaults on Christian faith and community. One of the most important was Justin Martyr (ca. 100–65), whose three extant works are all apologies. The *First Apology* and *Second Apology* address a Roman audience responsible for political persecution of Christians and *The Dialogue with*

*Trypho* addresses a Jewish audience.[4] To offer an example, in his *First Apology*, Justin begins by identifying criticisms made against the church by outsiders—atheism, immoral behavior, and not being loyal to the emperor. After addressing these particular accusations, Justin launches into an extensive defense of Christian faith as a rational philosophy, exploring parallel themes in Christian and non-Christian mythology and thought. While defending the faith against criticisms, Justin explains to Christians how their faith makes sense in terms adapted from the prevailing Greek philosophical worldview which they would have taken for granted.[5]

Once Constantine legalized Christianity (313), apologetics shifted from defending the minority faith against misunderstanding and accusations to arguing for the Christian faith as the best worldview over other alternatives. Augustine (354–430) is perhaps the best example of this approach. Having converted to Christianity from Manicheism, his early written works focused on refuting Manicheism (*On the Catholic and Manichean Ways of Life, Of True Religion, On the Usefulness of Belief*). While Augustine's writings over the course of his career covered a wide range of theological and ecclesial topics, across many of them he drew on Platonism to interpret the faith in ways that made sense in light of contemporaneous epistemology. And one of his greatest works, *The City of God against the Pagans*, defended a spiritual view of the faith (the city of God over the city of humanity) in light of accusations that Rome had been sacked by the Visigoths in 410 because of the Empire rejecting traditional Roman religion for Christianity.

---

4. The full English texts of Justin's writings can be found at Christian Classics Ethereal Library, http://www.ccel.org/ccel/schaff/anf01.viii.i.html.

5. Similar efforts that defend Christian faith while adding to its interpretation occur during the patristic period, e.g., second century: Aristides, *Apology*; Athenagoras, *Supplications for Christians;* third century: Clement of Alexandria, *Protrepticus;* Origen, *Contra Celsum;* Tertullian, *To the Pagan* and, of course, *Apology;* fourth century: Eusebius, *Preparation of the Gospel,* and *Proof of the Gospel.*

In the medieval period, apologetic theology began less by responding to direct attack from outsiders and more by thinkers perceiving threats to Christian faith posed by the two other Abrahamic movements—Judaism and Islam. In each case, Christian theologians seek both to discredit aspects of Judaism and Islam and to establish the reliability and superiority of Christianity. The title of a work by Peter the Venerable (ca. 1092–1156) reveals this approach: *Against the Inveterate Obstinacy of the Jews.* Unfortunately, such works contributed forcefully to anti-Semitism. Thomas Aquinas (1225–74) devoted extensive space to refuting his approximate Islamic contemporary, the learned Averroes. Averroes's interpretation of the rediscovered works of Aristotle had significant influence in European universities and was seen as a serious challenge to Christian theology. In *Summa Contra Gentiles*, Aquinas countered this influence by developing a Christian philosophy rooted in the very Aristotelian thought that had challenged the faith.

The Reformation and early Protestant movements were not greatly concerned with apologetic endeavors. This was for two main reasons. First, because Europe was overwhelmingly Christian, there were few outsiders against whom the church had to defend itself or to try to persuade. Second, and related to the first, the debates raging in Protestantism involved defining their stances over against Catholics or other Protestant movements instead of in relation to non-Christian worldviews.

## Modernism

Protestant engagement in apologetics, then, really began with the rise of the modern worldview, which began to come to expression in the late seventeenth century and challenged the Christian faith in radically different ways than it had been challenged in the past. The bulk of this chapter will describe three of the major apologetic responses to these developments. For now, then, let us examine only the challenges.

The Age of the Enlightenment brought with it a devotion to reason over against the church's emphasis on revelation passed on by communal tradition. While it inherited from the previous eras described above a view of truth and values as universal, modernity assumed truth could only be discovered and confirmed by human intellect. While a marked individuality was paired with this valuation of reason, reason was believed to have the ability to describe and prescribe universals that would lead to a homogenization in all aspects of life. Intellectuals, therefore, sought a reasonable foundation on which all knowledge could be built. Religious teachings, whether they be drawn from scripture or the Magisterium, could only be considered true if they corresponded to truth established by reason and founded on the same reasonable foundation as all knowledge.

Modernity's confidence in reason led to the expectation that humanity could finally make real, if not quite ultimate, progress in overcoming human hardship and suffering. Human ingenuity could raise the standard of living in ways never before imagined. Thus was born the industrial revolution followed by the information, technological, and digital revolutions.

Perhaps most significant to the coup d'état in which reason dethroned revelation, however, was the scientific revolution (which was both a precursor of and partner to the revolutions just mentioned). All types of thinking—economic, political, philosophical, theological, exegetical—aimed to be scientific in their methodologies. Make a hypothesis, gather evidence, and test the claim in order to try to verify it. One could recognize as true those things that could be demonstrated by empirical, objective observation. Historical reasoning is a prime example. The Enlightenment approach to historical research was to reconstruct a facts-only version of the past and reject as mythological any claims about the past that could not be reconciled with a scientific, rationalistic explanation.

The reason that empirical observation and scientific verification were so highly valued in modernity was that the world was considered to be reasonable in the sense that it operates in ways that can be scientifically observed, studied, and interpreted. Those who accepted the modern perspective thought that the world operates according to natural laws and that all things that happen in the natural world could be explained according to these laws. Sir Isaac Newton established this worldview so firmly in the late 1600s that there seemed to be little need for a providential God. God might have created the world, but God did not act in supernatural ways to keep it running. Science is always hungry to devour the next gap in knowledge, however, and eventually would even challenge the need for a creator. With Charles Darwin's theory of natural selection in the mid-nineteenth century and the development of the Big Bang theory in the early twentieth century, the need for a divine creator got smaller and smaller.

Christianity could not continue on as if the world around it had not changed. The church, especially the Protestant church, responded to the rise and development of modernism in a number of ways. The three primary responses that we will examine are to resist and debate the scientific worldview on the basis of revelation, adapt to the scientific worldview and reinterpret the Christian faith in ways that align with it, or argue the church's claims of truth are of a different sort than those claimed by the rest of the world.

## Postmodernism

We cannot only evaluate these three apologetic neighborhoods in relation to modernism, however, because the over three hundred-year-old modernist epistemology and worldview has been waning for over a half-century now. Postmodernism is on the ascendency. This new worldview potentially represents as dramatic an epistemological shift from modernism as did the transition from premodern to modern. One of the problems with naming the challenges that postmodernity represents for the church and its apologetic efforts is that it is evolving and may be fairly early in its evolution. For instance, it is unclear yet whether postmodernism will lead to a rejection of modernism or more of a modification of it. Still, some general patterns and tendencies are evident in terms of a fairly widespread "cultural postmodernism."[6]

One of the strongest impetuses for questioning modernism was World War II, and especially the Holocaust and the use of the atom bombs. These horrors not only continued to challenge the premodern view of a providential God in control of the world; they also challenged the humanistic valuation of reason in modernity. The hopes that progress wrought by reason and science would lead to solving humanity's problem were dashed when that very progress led to the mass slaughter of millions of Jews and to the ability to destroy whole populations with a single warhead.

While reason has not been fully abandoned in postmodernity, its search for a foundation of all human knowledge, and thus a universal perspective on truth, is considered to have failed. Postmodernism rejects the idea that any reasoning is objective. It views with significant suspicion top-down authority that makes any sort of absolute claim, assuming such claims are expressions of self-interest and assertions of power. Thus, the search for a universalized and homogenized worldview and

---

6. There are many works that detail the rise and characteristics of postmodernism. A few that are accessible and have an eye toward the Christian faith (including stances with which we would disagree) are Stanley J. Grenz, *A Primer on Postmodernism* (Grand Rapids: William B. Eerdmans, 1996); Paul Lakeland, *Postmodernity: Christian Identity in a Fragmented Age*, Guides to Theological Inquiry (Minneapolis: Fortress, 1997); Heath White, *Postmodernism 101: A First Course for the Curious Christian* (Grand Rapids: Brazos, 2006); and James K. A. Smith, *Who's Afraid of Postmodernism: Taking Derrida, Lyotard, and Foucault to Church* (Grand Rapids: Baker Academic, 2006). We borrow the term *cultural postmodernism* from Lakeland.

way of life has given way to embracing subjectivity, particularity, and diversity among individuals and communities. Modernity's emphasis on the individual's ability to reason as the primary authority for discovering universal truth has been replaced in many corners by individual *experience* as the primary authority for constructing contextual meaning, so that individualism has become even more rampant in Western society. Put differently, in response to the idea that all perception is interpretation (including conclusions reached by the scientific method and historical reasoning), many postmoderns no longer speak of *the* truth but honor the pluralism of many of the different ways that individuals and particular communities identify and practice what is most important to them relative to their perception of the world.

This shift represents a significant challenge to the Christian faith with its metanarrative extending from creation to eschatological consummation. The idea that the world has a singular purpose (*telos*) toward which God is drawing it is replaced by claims that meaning is assigned to the world by individuals, communities, and cultures. Acceptance of absolute religious claims like that found in the expression that Christ is *the* Way, *the* Truth, and *the* Life is frequently replaced with recognition that religious claims are multivalent, inviting multiple interpretations, and an eclectic approach to making meaning by drawing from a wide range of accessible resources—Christ is *a* way, *a* truth, *a* life.

The primary question of this book is *How shall the church and its preachers respond to the changing cultural contexts of postmodernity?* In what ways are the three broad theological and apologetic responses to modernity—the evangelical, liberal, and postliberal neighborhoods—appropriate or inappropriate for proclaiming the faith in a postmodern world to a postmodern audience?[7]

---

7. There are significant theological schools that we do not review in this chapter. Of special note are liberation and racial/ethnic theologies. With their focus on countering structural oppression and/or doing theology from a specific social location and experiential identity, these theologies have not been as concerned with questions related to apologetics as the schools discussed in the chapter. That said, libera-

# The Hatfields and the McCoys

A famous feud took place between the Hatfield and McCoy families in the late 1800s in Appalachia on the border between Kentucky and West Virginia. While the feud involved tension and violence, there were also moments of cooperation, humor, and even romance that crossed the family lines. This feud is a metaphor for the evangelical relationship with modernity (and postmodernity). For classical evangelicals, the feud is between faith (especially revelation in the form of the Bible and orthodox Christian doctrine) and reason (especially science and philosophy).[8] Like the feud between the Hatfields and the McCoys, this one also has moments when the two parties come together, if not in romance, at least in common concern.

## *Characteristics of the Theological Neighborhood*

For classical evangelicals, God revealed the essential elements of Christian faith by inspiring the content of the Bible. Traditional Christian doctrine clarifies, expands, and systematizes the revelation in the Bible. According to evangelicals, the content of the Bible and traditional Christian doctrine is factually true in scientific and philosophical senses. Indeed, this revelation must be true in order for it to be worthy of acceptance today.[9] As representative of this movement, we cite *Carl F. H. Henry*, one of the most influential figures in evangelicalism in the twentieth

---

tion and racial/ethnic theologians can be found living (with various levels of comfort) in each of the three neighborhoods.

8. We use the modifier *classical* to signify a recognition that there are many nuanced variations within evangelical circles, especially as evangelicalism is shifting in numerous directions today. (See our discussion in the next chapter.) Our goal in describing a classical evangelical position in the broad strokes we use is to set up clear contrasts for the proposal we will make in the following chapter, not to assert all evangelical individuals and communities are monolithic. The same approach will be used for our description of liberal and postliberal Christianity, and of our own conversational approach.

9. Of course, evangelicals acknowledge that the Bible contains figurative language. For example, when John the Baptist says of Jesus, "Here is the Lamb of God" (John 1:29), the evangelicals believe that John referred not to a wool-covered, four-footed animal, but to the human figure of Jesus (figuratively described as a lamb). Evangelicals themselves sometimes debate where to draw the line between the figurative and the literal. Evangelicals also debate how to arrange the various pieces of the Bible.

century. Henry explains that the Bible is the source of our knowledge of God. This knowledge comes in propositions that reveal God's nature and purposes and that point to the appropriate human response. The self-disclosure of God is found in only one place: the Bible.[10] Henry, like many evangelicals, explicitly lamented "the compromise of the authority of the Bible" to "modern speculations." His massive *God, Revelation and Authority* has a deep apologetic purpose, namely, to put forward a defense of the Bible and of traditional Christian doctrine.

From the evangelical standpoint, the contents of the Bible and orthodox Christian teaching are internally consistent, and they are valid in every time and place. The preacher and community may need to draw out the significance of the Bible and doctrine for particular circumstances, but the community can assume that the voices of tradition contain revelation that can guide the present.

To be sure, evangelicals differ among themselves regarding such things as the nature and extent of the inspiration of the Bible, the nature and degree of its inerrancy, where to draw the line between literal and figurative meanings of texts, and the degree the biblical writers or church councils might have contributed their own creativity to the Bible and Christian doctrine. In fact, evangelicals sometimes disagree regarding how to interpret and apply the Bible and Christian doctrine for today's world, resulting in the fact of different theological camps with different nuances in the evangelical world. However, beneath differences of opinion along these lines, classical evangelicals agree that because they come from God, the core of the Bible and Christian tradition are reliable, even necessary, guides for the continuing church.

Evangelicals use apologetics to defend their theological "land" against the incursions of modernity.[11] From an evangelical point of view,

---

10. Carl F. H. Henry, *God, Revelation, and Authority*, vol. 3 (Waco: Word, 1976), 468.

11. While our concern is with a classic evangelical position, it is important to note that this type of apologetic emphasis continues to have influence. Evangelical books on apologetics continue to appear

if the Bible is not historically accurate, and if the assertions of traditional beliefs are not reliable, then Christian faith collapses. Since God inspired the Bible, the content of the Bible must be correct, or people must admit that God was wrong in what God said in the Bible. Since, by definition, God cannot be wrong, the Bible must be true.

On a day-to-day basis, evangelicals value many things associated with the modern worldview such as developments in technology, medicine, political theory, and human rights. Indeed, in a broad sense, evangelicals and modernists hold the same view: truth is the correspondence of statement and reality and, thus, truth is absolute and universal.

The feud develops when evangelical convictions about revelation bump against the modern notion of the world as a place ruled by natural law and in which people accept as authoritative only those things confirmed by the scientific method. Evangelicals seek to show that the Bible and Christian doctrine are true in the sense that their claims are true, the events described in the biblical narratives *actually* took place, and today's congregation can embrace the declarations of the Bible and doctrine. They defend the factuality of biblical stories that tell of events that violate natural law and other aspects of the Enlightenment mentality, such as the Nile turning to blood, the Israelites crossing the Red Sea on dry ground, an axe head floating on the water, or the resurrection of a person from the dead.

The story of God creating the universe in six days, as found in Genesis 1, is a straightforward example of how classical evangelicals deal with a case in which the Bible and science appear to disagree. From an evangelical perspective, science is mistaken in concluding that the universe began with the "Big Bang" over thirteen billion years ago and life on

---

every year. Indeed, a long-time best seller has been Josh McDowell, *Evidence That Demands a Verdict: Historical Evidences for the Christian Faith* now reissued as *The New Evidence That Demands a Verdict* (Nashville: Thomas Nelson, 1999). Many evangelical Bible colleges and theological seminaries offer courses in apologetics. One of us is friends with a couple who conduct apologetics seminars in their congregation for students leaving for college so that the students can survive college with their evangelical faith intact.

earth (especially the human species) evolved through the process of natural selection over the course of some four billion years. The word *mistaken* is important here because, as noted, evangelicals do view science as making many positive contributions. But when the conclusions of modern science differ from viewpoints in the Bible, then contemporary people should reject the scientific conclusion in favor of knowledge revealed by God in the Bible and reinterpret the scientific evidence.

Apologetics is fundamental to the evangelical enterprise. In the image of the feud, the church regards the culture as an enemy when the beliefs and values of culture shaped by modernity disagree at crucial points with the Bible or traditional Christian doctrine. When dealing expressly with the relationship of Christian faith and aspects of modern culture, the classical evangelical church often uses the language of debate. The preacher seeks to establish the truth of the evangelical message over and against the claims of the culture. The preacher might try to show that evangelical perspectives make sense in ways that the scientific worldview would acknowledge.

Kenneth Boa and Robert M. Bowman, Jr. point out that the evangelical community works with not one but four broad approaches to apologetics. While a particular author or movement may emphasize one approach, many preachers and congregations employ more than one of these approaches.[12] The four approaches are the following:

- *Classical apologetics* uses logical criteria such as coherence, noncontradiction, self-consistency, and comprehensiveness to defend Christian assertions against modern challenges. The apologist makes a case that God exists and then shows that God revealed the divine purposes in the Bible.[13]

---

12. Kenneth D. Boa and Robert M. Bowman, Jr., *Faith Has Its Reasons: Integrative Approaches to Defending the Christian Faith* (Exeter: Paternoster, 2006), 34–36.

13. As representative of classical apologetics: Norman Giesler, *Christian Apologetics* (Grand Rapids: Baker Academic, 1988).

- *Evidentialism* is the explicit effort to show that the Christian faith is based on empirical facts that can be historically confirmed. Evidentialists marshal archaeology and other historical evidence to show that Christian claims broadly, and the material in the Bible narrowly, are believable on the basis of the same structure of probability that scientists use.[14]

- *Reformed apologetics*, sometimes called presuppositional apologetics, argues that the human mind is so corrupt or fallen that the church cannot trust reason alone be it in the form of science or classical and evidential apologetics. The world is not intelligible apart from the presupposition of believing in the God of the Bible.[15]

- *Fideism*—which comes from the Latin *fide*, "faith"—claims that the truth of Christian faith cannot be argued in a rational manner and that belief in God (and the Bible) cannot rely on logical reasoning or persuasive evidence. At their best, fideists show both why reason cannot provide an adequate basis for Christian faith and why the fideist position does furnish a compelling account for such belief.[16]

Of these four approaches, classical apologetics and evidentialism appear to be the most widely used in classical evangelical preaching. In actual practice, these two forms of apologetics are often combined in a single sermon, as in Haddon Robinson's case study sermon on the resurrection (below). Forms of fideism appear to be gaining ground, especially among newer evangelicals (often called neo-evangelicals).[17]

---

14. As representative of evidentialism: John Warwick Montgomery, *Faith Founded on Fact: Essays in Evidential Apologetics* (Nashville: Thomas Nelson, 1978).

15. As representative of this viewpoint: Cornelius Van Til, *Christian Apologetics*, 2nd ed. (Phillipsburg: Presbyterian and Reformed Publishing, 2003).

16. As representative of fideism: Donald G. Bloesch, *Essentials of Evangelical Theology, 2 vols. in 1* (Peabody, MA.: Hendrickson, 2006, o.p. 1978, 1982).

17. Fideism is similar to postliberalism (see below) in rejecting the need to defend its viewpoint against the challenges of modernity. However, evangelical fideism differs from postliberalism in the way that it views the Bible as divinely inspired.

Reformed apologetics are practiced largely by preachers in the conservative Reformed tradition.[18]

## *Apologetics in the Evangelical Pulpit*

Since the Bible contains divine guidance necessary for life, it is not surprising that evangelicals regard the Bible as essential for preaching. The evangelical preaching community contains differing nuances on apologetics and on the nature, purpose, and forms for preaching. However, *Haddon W. Robinson*, Professor of Preaching at Gordon Conwell Theological Seminary and author of the influential preaching textbook, *Biblical Preaching: The Development and Delivery of Expository Messages*, applies many of the themes common to classical evangelicals described above to the task of preaching. Central to his homiletic is the idea that God reveals God's self through scripture:

> God speaks through the Bible. It is the major tool of communication by which [God] addresses individuals today. Biblical preaching, therefore, must not be equated with "the old, old story of Jesus and his love"[19] as though it were retelling history about better times when God was alive and well. Nor is preaching merely a rehash of ideas about God—orthodox, but removed from life. Through the preaching of the Scriptures, God encounters men and women to bring them to salvation (2 Tim 3:15) and to richness and ripeness of Christian character (vv. 16-17).[20]

Robinson continues, "The type of preaching that best carries the force of divine authority is expository preaching."[21] This type of preach-

---

18. While the apologetic task is central to classical evangelical theology, many evangelical preachers *assume* the results of apologetics from Sunday to Sunday without defending them. That is, they preach as if the congregation knows and accepts the results of apologetic arguments without feeling the need to have an expressly apologetic element in every sermon. Nevertheless, from time to time, many evangelical preachers bring apologetics into the sermon.

19. Katherine Hankey, "I Love to Tell the Story," *The United Methodist Hymnal* (Nashville: The United Methodist Publishing House, 1989), 156.

20. Haddon W. Robinson, *Biblical Preaching: The Development and Delivery of Expository Messages*, 3rd ed. (Grand Rapids: Baker Academic, 2014), 4.

21. Ibid.

ing is "the communication of a biblical concept, derived from and trans-
mitted through a historical, grammatical, and literary study of a passage
in its context, in which the Holy Spirit first applies to the personality
and experience of the preacher, then, through the preacher, applies to the
hearers."[22] The passage, then, should govern the sermon. The preacher
must listen to the passage and turn away from theological constructs
(no matter how cherished) that make theological claims that differ from
the passage. The preacher then draws a central concept or proposition, a
big idea from the passage itself, around which the sermon coheres, and
which preachers apply to themselves and to the hearers.[23]

Preachers must do three things in a sermon:[24]

We explain it: "What does it mean?"

We prove it: "Is it true?"

We apply it: "What difference does it make?"

Our immediate interest, of course, is in number two: "We prove it:
'Is it true?'" From Robinson's perspective, apologetics is at the heart of
preaching: "An initial response of those of us who take the Scriptures
seriously is to ignore this question. We assume that an idea should be accepted as true because it comes from the Bible. That is not necessarily a
valid assumption. We may need to gain psychological acceptance in our
hearers through reasoning, proofs, or illustrations."[25]

The preacher does not "establish biblical truth" by means of scientific analysis or philosophical reasons but rather uses such means

---

22. Ibid., 5.

23. Ibid., 5ff.

24. Ibid., 50–66.

25. Ibid., 53.

to reinforce the congregation's confidence in "the truth taught in Scripture."[26]

The preacher should respond to the question, "Is that true? Do I really believe it?" For example, how can a congregation believe that "all things work together for good" for those who love Christ (Rom 8:28) in the face of a mother who was killed in a tragic automobile accident? To fail to deal with such questions is "to miss the audience completely."[27] The consequence of ignoring the apologetic element may not only be that the congregation does not take seriously the claims of the text and the sermon, but worse, "because we have not been willing to lie for a time on the sloping back of a question mark, we [preachers] may become hucksters for a message we do not believe ourselves."[28]

This apologetic approach is exemplified in a sermon on the resurrection Professor Robinson preached in a congregation on an Easter Sunday.[29] The introduction to the sermon raises the claim to be defended immediately by telling about a novel in which a group of archaeologists faked the discovery of the body of Jesus. When this news broke, Christians lost faith, churches closed, and missionaries came home. The preacher then forthrightly states the big idea of the sermon. "Of one thing I am certain. The author of that novel understood the heartbeat of the Christian faith. For if the body of Jesus were found rotted in a Palestinian grave, Christianity would crumble. The firm foundation of the Christian faith rests on an empty tomb."[30]

---

26. Ibid., 55.

27. Ibid.

28. Ibid., 57.

29. The sermon is found at http://media.mbcokc.com/messages/audio/3006.01.mp3. Accessed June 23, 2014. All references to the sermon that follow are from this recording.

30. Although the gospel accounts of the resurrection as well as other pertinent texts from the Gospels and Letters are in the background of much of Robinson's sermon, he makes relatively few explicit references to biblical texts in the sermon and fails to offer an exposition of a passage in any detail. In other words, he gives the apologetic methods of classical and evidentialist apologetics priority over biblical exposition in this sermon.

Professor Robinson raises the question directly. "What evidence do Christians have . . . that Jesus Christ rose physically from the dead?" The preacher states that of "the many lines of evidence," he will bring three forward. The preacher majors in classical apologetics with a touch of evidentialism.

The first line of evidence is the integrity of the witnesses. In a court case, you want witnesses with character and integrity. Jesus was such a witness: he predicted his own death and resurrection thirteen times. The witnesses to the resurrection also have integrity. The united and impressive testimony of the disciples is that they saw Jesus alive after the resurrection.

According to Robinson, the second line of evidence is the reality of the empty tomb. Virtually everyone agrees that the tomb did not contain a body on that Easter morning. What happened to the body? The disciples could not have stolen it. Archaeology tells us that such stones were massive slabs that could only be moved with great difficulty. The disciples could hardly have bypassed the Roman soldiers to steal the body. Furthermore, the grave bore the Roman seal. Robinson vividly says, "If a [person] broke the Roman seal, Rome broke the person." Moreover, the enemies of Jesus would not have stolen the body. They wanted Jesus in the grave to be rid of him. To silence the resurrection message, the enemies of Jesus had only to produce the body. Yet, they could not.

To show the trustworthy nature of this evidence, Robinson appeals to the contemporary testimony of people whom the congregation might identify as authorities. Frank Morrison, a British agnostic and newspaper reporter, sought to debunk the story of the resurrection. Morrison hypothesized that after three hours on the cross, Jesus appeared to be dead, but when the body was placed in the tomb, the cool air revived him. But David Friedrich Strauss claimed that it is more difficult to believe in such explanations than it is to believe in the resurrection itself.

Would a professional executioner be misled by the condition of the body on the cross? Would a revived Jesus be able to push away the massive stone? After appearing to the disciples, would Jesus find another grave and close it on himself so the disciples would believe he had ascended? Such explanations of the resurrection are hardly credible.

The third line of evidence, according to Robinson, is almost invincible: the resurrection resulted in the transformation of the followers of Jesus. People in antiquity doubted the resurrection. Yet, the followers of Jesus claimed again and again that Jesus was raised. People may preach a lie when it puts gold in their pockets, but they do not do so when such preaching leads to persecution: mocked by friends, crucified upside down (Peter), boiled in oil (John), and others turned into torches in Nero's circus.

Robinson then, again, follows up the description of antiquity with contemporary appeals to the testimony of people who "have looked closely at the historic record." Robinson cites several thinkers who offer reasons for believing in the resurrection. Thomas Arnold, who wrote a three-volume history of Rome and taught at Oxford, said he knows of nothing in history better attested than the resurrection of Jesus. Samuel Greenleaf, an expert in trial evidence, attests to the persuasive character of the evidence. Frank Morison was a writer who intended to write a book arguing that the stories of the resurrection of Jesus have no basis, but in the process he came to believe in the resurrection and wrote the book *Who Moved the Stone?*[31]

Professor Robinson concludes the sermon by applying confidence in the resurrection to the congregation. Here the apologetic element recedes. Robinson asks, "What difference does it make to believe in the resurrection of Jesus Christ?" The difference is eternal. According to Romans 4:25, Jesus's death removed the great barrier between God and us:

31. Frank Morison, *Who Moved the Stone?* (London: Faber and Faber, 1938).

sin. But, how do you know that Jesus's death settled the problem of sin? When God raised Jesus from the dead, God announced that God was satisfied with Jesus's death. The resurrection is God's "signed receipt" that the death of Jesus has taken away sin. "All we have to do is be satisfied with that which satisfies God."

The first consequence of the resurrection, then, is that "all your guilt has been completely removed." A second consequence is that one who trusts in Jesus Christ has a relationship with a savior who is alive. The New Testament proclaims this message. "I live by the power of Jesus Christ who indwells me." Robinson makes a stirring affirmation that the listeners can be all that God created them to be as a result of a relationship with the living Christ. The sermon closes with an appeal to the listeners to come and put their trust in Christ.

Robinson illustrates evangelical apologetics by marshaling arguments and evidence claiming the resurrection is believable in a modern setting. At one level, there is continuity between the preacher's homiletical theory and the sermon in that the sermon develops a big idea, a proposition: when we believe in the truth of the resurrection, we can be certain of individual salvation in the ways named in the application. At another level, however, there is a disconnect. The sermon is more a topical discussion of the resurrection than the exposition of a text or texts. Moreover, the apologetic does not directly determine the application given. The truth of the resurrection could be the basis of any number of applications.

## Critical Reflection on Evangelical Preaching and Apologetics

Classical evangelical approaches to apologetics have several strengths. Evangelicals are clear about their understanding of the content of Christian faith and its differences from other ways of understanding the self and world. In our view, one of the greatest strengths of evangelical apologetic preaching is that it gives the congregation the opportunity not only to be clear about *what* they can believe but also *why* they do so. While this aspect of evangelical apologetics came to birth in response to the Enlightenment mentality, it is important in the increasingly pluralism and diversity of emerging postmodernity. Indeed, while other theological neighborhoods have different methods and standards for truth, and may even abandon the category of truth itself, evangelical apologetics reminds all Christians of the importance of coming to clarity and confidence in what we most deeply believe about the nature of God and God's purposes for the world.

Evangelical apologetics make use of methods of determining truth that are familiar to people influenced by the modern ways of thinking, as for example, in appealing to evidence on which the congregation needs to render its own verdict. In this context, the preacher has a clear assignment: to identify the truth at the center of the text, show why the congregation can believe that truth amid the acids of modernity (and emerging postmodernity), and apply it to the congregation and its context. This sometimes means that the congregation must take a stand against modern assumptions.

The evangelical confidence in the Bible as the revelation of God offers the congregation a feeling of security in the midst of an increasingly pluralistic and sometimes confusing and contradictory postmodern ethos. The evangelical notion of the unity of the Bible gives the preacher a way to make sense of the many parts of the Bible that seem to differ from one another. The different kinds of apologetics (e.g. classical, evidential, Reformed, fideist) offer preachers a range of apologetic approaches to coordinate with different congregations or different purposes. Moreover, the preacher has access to a vast amount of literature on evangelical apologetics to help with the apologetic sermon.

At the same time, the classical evangelical approach to apologetics faces important questions. Evangelicals walk a fine line in their relationship with modernity. As noted earlier, classical evangelicals subscribe to the modern notion that for statements to be true (and, therefore, reliable), statements must be empirically verified or must cohere with foundational first principles. Evangelical apologists are often careful to say that they do not make the truth of the Bible attendant on empirical verification. Rather, empirical verification only shows that the Bible is true. Nevertheless, the preacher is perilously close to letting science and reason judge the truth of the Bible. In a sense, this stance allows the modern standard for truth to become the standard by which evangelical congregations measure truth. Evangelical preaching is supposed to center in exposition of the biblical text with appropriate application for today. The preacher is to listen for what the text asks the congregation to believe and do, and then to help the congregation recognize how these things relate today. Indeed, preachers need to be open to reformulating aspects of their theologies when their constructs disagree with texts. However, evangelical preachers do not always engage in serious exposition of a particular text. For example, while the sermon on the resurrection by Haddon Robinson (above) assumes the resurrection stories in the Gospels, it does not expound any one text. In such circumstances, ministers put forward a doctrinally acceptable message but lose the opportunity to do so in light of the particularity of the text.

While evangelicals typically claim that the Bible is the sole standard for determining faith and practice, the Bible assumes some values that run against the grain of contemporary experience and sensibility. For example, while the Bible may contain impulses against such things, the Bible in broad view assumes the validity of slavery and a patriarchal social order in which women are subordinate to men. No evangelicals in North America would defend the validity of slavery and increasing numbers of evangelicals acknowledge the egalitarianism of women and men in the workplace, if not always in the church. From an outsider's point of view, such efforts seem to be sparked by awareness that the experience of slaves and of women is often abusive. Evangelicals may find ways of interpreting the Bible that critique slavery and patriarchy, but, to our knowledge, evangelicals seldom acknowledge the role of experience in raising such issues.

To many readers, the Bible appears to be diverse not only in the times and places in which documents were written and in literary genres, but also in theological claims. While classical evangelicals have ways of explaining this diversity, in our view, such explanations do not adequately account for differences. Moreover, they are willing to use the Bible as evidence for their apologetics without answering the challenges of historical criticism that would claim such "evidence" is theological and not historical in nature.

Some people describe evangelicalism as premodern. In fact, evangelicalism in its modern form originated in response to modern questions and issues. An irony here, however, is that evangelicals apologetically use modern methods to defend a faith whose theological content is premodern. This situation creates a tension in which believers can be modern in every way but one, the one that matters most. Over the years, the feud between the Hatfields and the McCoys has resulted in not a few funerals. Similarly, the feud between faith and reason leaves any person desiring to embrace a modern worldview fully to bury the Christian faith as having died in the past.

## Apartment Dwelling

The classical liberal response to modernity is to think of the church along the lines of an apartment dweller.[32] In an apartment building, the

32. As we did with "classical evangelicalism," here we use the modifier *classical* to signify a recogni-

tenant pays rent to the owner alongside other residents paying the same rent to the same landlord. In the liberal church, faith pays rent to reason. That is, the church accommodates its understanding of the Bible, doctrine, and ethics to the rational modern worldview. The terms of the lease can change as the modern worldview evolves: the owner has the upper hand, and the church modifies its faith on the basis of developments in scientific or philosophical perspective. The position is more "in the world" than "not of the world."

In common parlance today, "liberal" is synonymous with progressive and is contrasted with conservative. We are using it instead in the historical sense of the word (as in "liberal arts" education). From the perspective of the Enlightenment, the worldview of premodern people was dominated by unscientifically proven tradition, and characterized by such things as superstition and the arbitrary exercise of authority by religious and political authorities. Human intellect was in darkness (e.g., the "Dark" Ages) until the Enlightenment was able to liberate people through the standards of human reason.

The liberal theological neighborhood, therefore, intends to liberate the church from superstition that is dependent upon domination by ancient and outdated authorities. Liberal theologians move out of the apartment complex owned by scripture and tradition to the one owned by reason and experience. While there were other theologians trying to reconcile the Christian faith with the Enlightenment before him, the theologian who is usually credited as the most influential in leading others to this new neighborhood was *Friedrich Schleiermacher* (1768–1834). His *On Religion: Speeches to Its Cultured Despisers* was the

---

tion that there are many nuanced variations within liberal circles, especially as liberalism is shifting in numerous directions today. Our goal in describing a liberal position in the broad strokes we use is to set up clear contrasts for the proposal we will make in the following chapter, not to assert all liberal individuals and communities are monolithic. The same approach will be used for our description of postliberal Christianity and of our own conversational approach.

map.[33] Whereas educated people were inclined to view religion rooted in revelation as passé, Schleiermacher argued that religion was grounded in human nature, that is, in a universal human experience, intuition, or feeling of the Divine. Classical liberals following Schleiermacher share with evangelicals a common concern for people to have confidence in faith within the criteria of modernity. Both communities accept the Enlightenment perspective that human knowledge is based on objectively real foundations (especially empirical verification and first principles) behind the Bible and doctrine. But whereas evangelicals seek to use modern views and methods to defend the historicity of the Bible and traditional Christian doctrine against modernity (revelation over reason), liberals adapt how they understand and apply the Bible and Christian doctrine to beliefs and moral behavior that are at home in modernity (reason over revelation).

Similarly, for both evangelicals and liberals, truth is universal and absolute. When either group encounters something in the Bible or traditional Christian faith and practice that runs counter to a modern claim, something has to give. But whereas evangelicals assume what has to give is the modern claim, liberals assume the problem is with the ancient claim. When liberals encounter a conflict between the views of the Bible and modernity, they typically seek to reconcile the two, often by recasting their understanding of the ancient Bible or doctrine according to modern forms of thought.

Whereas evangelicals recognize only one source of theological authority, the Bible, liberal apologetics recognizes multiple sources of authority. Among these resources are the Bible, Christian tradition and theology, science and philosophy, and the broader range of human experience. Moreover, liberals acknowledge a diversity of (and sometimes conflicting) voices within these authorities, especially in the Bible and

---

33. Friedrich Schleiermacher, *On Religion: Speeches to Its Cultured Despisers,* Cambridge Texts in the History of Philosophy (Cambridge: Cambridge University Press, 1996).

Christian tradition. From text to text and doctrine to doctrine, liberals weigh the different sources according to how they help the church articulate a genuinely modern faith.

Liberals are able to take this approach because they view the Bible as authored by human beings, as diverse in theological and ethical perspectives, and as requiring interpretation in dialogue with modern standards. This neighborhood uses historical criticism to explore how the biblical authors shaped the biblical materials as well as the diversity and functions of the biblical materials instead of assuming the historical and scientific veracity of scripture as given by God.

For liberals, there is a "hermeneutical gap" between the premodern (mythological) world of the Bible and the contemporary worldview. A purpose of theology is to find a bridge across this gap that moderns can cross. We note the four main ways that liberals cross this bridge in our comments on preaching below.

We can see these classical liberal themes in operation in two of the best known modern theologians of the twentieth century, *Rudolf Bultmann* and *Paul Tillich*. These thinkers' deep intent is apologetic. They want to offer modern people a faith in which they can truly believe and reconcile with a scientific understanding of the world. While the specific theological content of the work of Bultmann and Tillich differs in nuance, the structure of their theological thinking is similar.

Rudolf Bultmann shares the modern view that much of the premodern language of the Bible is mythological. In this sense, a myth is not simply a falsehood, as when one of our children makes a statement and we respond, "That is a myth," meaning, "You are not telling the truth." Rather, a myth is a story or other expression cast in the language of the worldview of antiquity that explains how ancient people experienced meaning in the world. Ancient people, for instance, believed in a three-story universe (heaven above, earth in the middle, and hell below) populated by angels and demons. Thus, Bultmann says that "it is impossible to repristinate a past world picture by sheer resolve, especially a *mythical* world picture, now that all of our thinking is irrevocably formed by science. A blind acceptance of New Testament mythology would be simply arbitrariness; to make such acceptance a demand of faith would be to reduce faith to a work."[34]

Bultmann's positive apologetic move is called "demythologizing." The relationship between the language of the Bible and its significance is like that of a husk to an ear of corn. The mythological language is the husk within which is a meaning that is not limited to its premodern dimensions. Behind the mythic world picture of the Bible is the kerygma, the ear of corn: the announcement of what potential life in God can be.

Bultmann translated the basic Christian message into the philosophical categories of existentialism, a movement in which individuals choose the basic values and practices that form their existence. We are not simply made up of the essence of beliefs, values, groups, and practices that we inherit, but we choose how we live. Bultmann wants us to decide in favor of the life that God reveals through Christ.

Like Bultmann, Tillich intends to put forward an interpretation of the Christian faith in which modern people can truly believe and that is truly meaningful. Tillich's modern approach can be seen in his famous hermeneutical method of correlation.[35] Tillich described the traditions of scripture and ancient Christianity as symbolic (similar to Bultmann's emphasis on myth). While the ancient trappings of these symbols cannot be taken literally in the modern era, people can and should hold onto the reality in which the symbols participate. Tillich identifies the philosophical and theological questions on the hearts and minds of the contemporary age. He then responds by correlating the symbolic an-

---

34. Rudolf Bultmann, *New Testament and Mythology and Other Basic Writings*, ed. Schubert M. Ogden (Philadelphia: Fortress, 1984), 3.

35. Paul Tillich, *Systematic Theology*, vol. 1 (Chicago: University of Chicago Press, 1951), 59–66.

swers found in the core of the Bible and Christian tradition with these questions, translating them as answers into categories of being, that is, categories with which the modern community can identify. For example, Tillich correlated the symbol of "God" with the Ground of Being and the symbols of resurrection and New Being with the question of authentic existence. Viewing sin as a symbol for alienation, he, in turn, described the biblical notion of grace as analogous to the contemporary experience of acceptance. Indeed, one of Tillich's most famous sermons is entitled "You Are Accepted," the point of which is to call the congregation to authentic existence as they would accept the fact that they are accepted by God.[36]

The classical liberal apologetic posture that descends from Schleiermacher, Bultmann, and Tillich can be illustrated in relation to the stories of creation in Genesis 1 and 2. Whereas a classical evangelical apologist would want to portray the events in the narratives as actually taking place in the way described, a liberal apologist observes that Genesis 1:1–2:4 and Genesis 2:5-25 are two separate narratives of the creation. Neither story comports with contemporary scientific explanations of the origins of the world. However, rather than dismiss the stories, liberals note that each story is cast in mythological/symbolic language and seek to identify the core theological concern expressed through such language that is still meaningful for people today. In other words, liberals are concerned with the theological truths underneath the mythology instead of any historical facts the creation stories seem to reference.

Working in this vein, liberals often view scientific language and religious language as having two different purposes. Science describes the way things are. Religion interprets the meaning of things. Genesis 1, then, on the surface seems to be describing the fact that God is the creator of the world and the method(s) by which God created. Underneath

---

36. Tillich, *The Shaking of the Foundations* (New York: Charles Scribner's Sons, 1948), 153–63.

this mythological description, however, are the theological claims that God is the source of all life and thus the One who gives purpose to the world—to be a community of love, peace, justice, and abundance.

### Liberalism in the Pulpit

Apologetic preaching in the liberal apartment building follows the overarching concern and movement of the classical liberal theological tradition.[37] From Bultmann's point of view, the vocation of the preacher is to demythologize the biblical text, that is, (1) to identify and strip away mythological overlay, (2) to identify the abiding element(s) of kerygma at the center, and (3) to call members of the congregation to make a decision to shape their existence according to the kerygma. As implied earlier, the purposes of preaching include encouraging people to decide to accept what God has done and to live accordingly. For Tillich the work of the preacher is similar: the preacher correlates today's questions with the resources of Christian faith as reinterpreted through the lens of contemporary philosophical categories.

While few liberal preachers adhere strictly with either Bultmann's or Tillich's hermeneutics, they typically follow one of (or some combination of) three apologetic strategies that are similar in basic orientation to the gap between the premodern past and modern present. First, liberals face the apologetic issue directly by pointing out that an ancient text or doctrine asks people to believe or do something that is no longer credible from a modern perspective. Having unmasked what moderns cannot believe, the preacher then translates the meaning behind the text into what moderns can believe.

Second, liberal preachers do sometimes deal directly with texts that appear to be straightforward and not encased in a mythological husk,

---

37. Our impression is that much, perhaps most, of the preaching in the historic denominations follows this liberal pattern, often supplemented by newer theological movements such as liberation theologies.

especially ethical passages. Still, some work in bridging the gap between the way an ethical principle would be employed in the ancient word and the way it should be employed in modernity must be undertaken. For example, in the case of "Love your neighbor as yourself" (Matt 22:39), the liberal preacher would likely explore what the concept of neighbor meant in antiquity and today, as well as what it meant to love one's neighbor then and what it might mean today. Indeed, instead of following the sort of existentialist hermeneutics seen in Bultmann or Tillich, liberal preachers often lean toward translating the mythological elements of scripture in ethical terms influenced by the Social Gospel movement.[38]

Third, liberal preachers often bridge the gap between the ancient and the contemporary by translating the Christian message into modern idioms. Preachers do this work of translation by drawing analogies between the ancient and contemporary worlds, especially between the situation in or behind the biblical text and the situation(s) faced by contemporary hearers. While they recognize that the cultures and worldviews of the ancient and contemporary communities are quite different, classical liberal preachers see these differences as being at the surface level. Underneath, the communities share deep levels of experience that are similar. In other words, the human condition and the experience of the Divine in the midst of that condition is the same in spite of the radically different ways the human condition manifests itself in antiquity and modernity. As the ancient text invited a certain experience of the kerygma in the situations it addressed, so are modern preachers to offer that same experience in the different situations they address.

In the last forty years, the New Homiletic has been especially influential in the liberal sermon's shift away from the exploration of an idea and more toward creating for the congregation an experience that

---

38. A prime example of this homiletical approach is William Sloane Coffin. See *The Collected Sermons of William Sloane Coffin*, 2 vols. (Louisville: Westminster John Knox, 2008) for resurrection sermons that make the move of translating ancient texts into Social Gospel concerns, see 1.67–71, 1.535–38, 2.155–59.

is analogous to that which is seen in the text. Rather than directly defending or translating the theological ideas or passages in the Bible into modern theological propositions, liberal preachers often turn to figurative speech—such as metaphor and story—to suggest theological interpretation in the context of the congregation experiencing the sermon.

Fred B. Craddock's groundbreaking work, *As One without Authority*, dwells comfortably in this New Homiletic's liberal apartment.[39] With his leaning on the existentialist theology of Søren Kierkegaard, it is easy to recognize that he is heir to the apologetic moves made by Tillich and Bultmann (and especially Bultmann's students in the New Hermeneutic).[40] In the 1960s, preaching was seen as in decline. As Craddock describes this decline, he includes two issues that are specifically related to the apologetic task. First, much of traditional theological language has lost its power and needs to be laid aside. Second, he does not deal with the claims of science against tradition, but with the way the language of science has overshadowed theological language for naming the world.[41]

Craddock's primary concern was to shift away from propositional preaching that flows in a deductive manner to an inductive flow that creates an experience of the gospel for the hearer and ends without a specific application, allowing the hearers the freedom to "apply" the gospel to their lives and worldview as they see fit. This is an apologetically motivated strategy. Translating a text's function not into a truth claim that has to be defended but into an experience to which the hearers relate as they see appropriately through the use of evocative, figurative lan-

39. Fred B. Craddock, *As One without Authority* (Nashville: Abingdon Press, 1971).

40. Craddock is more explicit about the influence of Kierkegaard on his work in *Overhearing the Gospel: Preaching and Teaching the Faith to Persons Who Have Heard It All Before* (Nashville: Abingdon Press, 1978).

41. Craddock, *As One without Authority*, 7–8.

guage, authorizes the hearers to determine the plausibility and relevance of Christian faith individually.

An example of this inductive, apologetic approach can be found in Craddock's Easter sermon, "The Announcement," based on Mark 16:1-8.[42] In it he tells the hearers that he, as a guest preacher, has come simply to make an announcement that God has raised Jesus from the dead.

The sermon begins with the experience of the difficulty of hearing such announcements and then moves to the difficulty of hearing this specific one. Craddock shows that it has always been a difficult announcement to hear by walking through the different Gospel versions of the Easter morning announcements and highlighting the initial responses of disbelief. Note that Craddock is not concerned with reconciling the differences in the stories that would concern a classical evangelical preacher trying to argue for the historicity of the resurrection. Instead, underneath the differences in details, he points out a shared experience—difficulty in hearing the Easter announcement.

Craddock concludes this section of the sermon with the following:

> I'm not going to trivialize [this announcement] by just speaking of eggs and flowers and daffodils and things. No, no. . . . My job is simply to make the announcement. And the announcement: Sometime this morning before first light, God raised Jesus of Nazareth from the dead. I can't, I can't shrink it by giving you a few minutes of explanation as to what resurrection means. I'm not going to shrink it by trying to give you scientific parallels so that it will help your believing.[43]

It is at this point that we see that Craddock's use of a contemporary time reference in the announcement is more than just a homiletical device. He rejects the kind of strategy of defending the historicity of the resurrection we saw in Robinson's sermon. Instead, his interest is in a

---

42. Craddock, *The Collected Sermons of Fred B. Craddock* (Louisville: Westminster John Knox, 2011), 103–8.

43. Ibid., 104.

contemporary experience of the resurrection: *This morning* God raised Jesus from the dead.

In the next section of the sermon, Craddock describes some who heard the Easter announcement as important for their lives and actions even though it was difficult to hear. John of Patmos in his exile in the face of Roman power and the Apostle Paul with his abused and painful body, groaning in their suffering, heard the announcement and persevered. Craddock explicitly refuses to exhort his hearers to persevere, keep the faith, and do good works in the midst of their struggles, but clearly he hopes this is the connection the hearer will make. He asks, "Why is it so that the more we live and become qualified to live, the more we live and become qualified to witness for our faith, the body won't go? Some of the finest volunteers I've ever known in the church were on walkers, in wheel chairs, and groaning. . . . But, you will have to make of the announcement what you will."[44] The apologetical move in this section is subtle but clear: the experience of the ancient announcement of the resurrection has been translated into the experience of persevering faith in contemporary life—living faithfully each day in the face of the power of death.

Even though earlier Craddock said he would not give "a few minutes of explanation as to what resurrection means," he does take on the tone of testimony and unpack this last move by naming explicitly that the resurrection is important specifically because God raises Jesus of Nazareth and not someone else.[45] He goes on to give examples of contemporary people who have not followed the example of John and Paul in persevering in the faith. They saw some aspect of the life of faith as too difficult and traded it off for something easier, to which Craddock offers the good news:

> I want everybody who's traded it off to know that God has vindicated this life, Jesus of Nazareth. Look at him. Nonviolent, never violent, turn

44. Ibid., 105.
45. Ibid., 105–6.

the other cheek, love your enemies. "How often must I forgive, Jesus? Seven times?" "No, no, no, seventy times seven." "But when I get kicked in the groin time and time and time again . . . I don't need this!" I want you to understand this is the life that God has raised from the dead and said, "Look, this is what I had in mind."[46]

In essence, what Craddock has done is translate the resurrection of the dead into lifting up Jesus as the model for perseverance in the life of faith. Living out the resurrection is, like Jesus, taking up your cross.[47] Bultmann or Tillich might say that he has translated the resurrection into the call to live into the potential for authentic existence.

Indeed, the sermon ends with a section in which Craddock extends this call implicitly by acknowledging that it takes some people longer to hear the Easter announcement than others. He provides a positive example of someone who took a long time to respond, and then concludes by saying that "my assignment is simply to announce to you that this morning sometime before sunrise, God raised from among the dead, Jesus of Nazareth. You have fifty days. In fact, I'm sure if you applied, you could get an extension."[48] In typical liberal fashion, Craddock's apologetic strategy in this sermon is to take the central claim of the Christian faith (resurrection) that is at odds with the Enlightenment worldview (dead is dead) and translate it into something believable, that is, into something *I* can do and be (i.e., I can live faithfully in the face of the deadly powers of the world).

## Critical Reflection on Liberal Apologetic Preaching

The great strength of apologetic preaching in the classical liberal apartment building is that it offers the community a faith that is at home in the modern worldview. It makes modern theological sense out

---

46. Ibid. 106–7.

47. Ibid., 107.

48. Ibid., 108.

of biblical materials and aspects of doctrine so that Christians can hold onto them and, at the same time, recognize the validity of evolutionary biology and such. It names and critiques aspects of the biblical tradition that do not fit in the modern worldview; it says clearly, "We, today, do not have to believe things from the past that are not credible from the perspective of the modern world in order to be Christian." For many people, this word is liberating.

Beyond that, the best liberal thinking does not leave people hanging out a tenth-story window with nothing to grab as it also articulates what we can believe about God's presence and activity, and, consequently, what we can count on from God and what is our responsibility.

Similarly, liberal apologetics allows the church to engage a broad range of sources in making sense of the world and the meaning of human existence—the Bible, Christian tradition, science, philosophy, and broader human experience. Within this broad spectrum, liberals can honor the diversity of the Bible. The best liberals draw on such sources to articulate a theological worldview that transcends any one biblical text or traditional statement of doctrine and is plausible in modern culture.

At the same time, liberal preaching often has a concern for social justice that runs counter to modern tendencies.[49] Liberals often call for God's universal desire for justice against industrial and technological advances that oppress our neighbors and put the planet in jeopardy. Because liberal preaching has bridged the gap between the ancient and the contemporary in terms of knowledge of God, world, and humanity, its ethical claims drawn from the ancient sources have a relevance for modern society that is easier to defend than similar or differing ethical claims made from the feuding posture of the evangelical pulpit.

---

49. Indeed, modern attitudes could be put to work in deeply regrettable ways. For example, Carl Linnaeus's classification of all living things included races. This taxonomy facilitated claims of racial superiority on the part of Eurocentric peoples over Afrocentric peoples and of Aryans over Jewish people.

However, challenges knock on the door of liberal apologetics. One important issue is that the conclusions of science and reason are not the fixed and firm foundations that many claimed in earlier generations (and some even today). Science sometimes revises its conclusions in response to new data and fresh perspectives on old data. Indeed, science itself is a kind of mythology. In one of the congregations in which one of us served, a layperson asked this question after a discussion of a liberal approach to a text, and the changing perspectives of science: "Well, then, if you are going to revise your theology after every report from the National Science Foundation, what can I count on from God?" The landlord, reason, can raise its rent at any time, and the church gets left with a God of the gaps, of smaller and smaller gaps.

Similarly, liberals must face the growing awareness in our postmodern culture that there is no such thing as objective knowledge, that we do not have pure, uninterpreted awareness. All perception is relative because it all takes place through lenses that reflect their social construction. This phenomenon is true even of simple empirical observation. While the authors of this volume believe that there are ontological and philosophical foundations on which knowledge sits, we do not have pure and objective access to those foundations. We can become as conscious and critical as we can of our own perceptual constructs, but we can never have 100 percent confidence in our perception. Even science is recognized to be a subjective discipline, so how much more true is this of Christian theology and proclamation that strives to take account of the developments of science.

On the liberal hermeneutical bridge (from the ancient text to the contemporary world), the traffic tends to run one way. As in the evangelical neighborhood, the liberal preacher and congregation largely *assume* the text has something positive to contribute to today's church. Liberals have been willing to critique the mythological husk but not the theological, existential, and experiential kernel. Because of their propensity to look for a positive meaning in every text, too often liberals strive to find kerygma in texts that raise difficult theological and ethical issues that should instead be critiqued from a modern or postmodern perspective. The liberal theological and ethical instinct often runs on two parallel rails that can lead to abuse. One on rail, liberals have theological and ethical instincts for universal love and justice. On the other rail, liberals want the existential significance underneath the mythology of the Bible to support their theological and ethical positions. The latter instinct sometimes prompts liberals to manipulate the Bible in ways that cross (or test) the boundaries of plausible exegetical interpretation. In their desire to be theologically appropriate and biblically based, liberal apologists sometimes remake the Bible in their own images.[50]

In more postmodern language, liberal preachers do not always respect the category of otherness. In terms of the otherness of scripture, for instance, the text is easily translated into modern terms and, thus, sometimes loses its power to engage individuals and communities in confrontational and transformative ways. In terms of the relation between the preacher and the members of the congregation, the assumption that the preacher's experience is, can, or should be shared by all hearing the sermon minimizes the differences in ways others experience God, world, church, and self.

In the process of accommodating biblical and theological perspectives to the modern world, the church sometimes loses some of the distinctive elements of its faith and message. This occurs especially when the preacher, in the name of accommodation, reduces the values and practices of the text to those of modernity. Whereas the feuding mentality of evangelical apologetics often finds too little common ground between the church and the world, the liberal approach sometimes shapes a

---

50. To be sure, exegetical discoveries do offer preachers opportunities to reread texts in ways that are more loving and just than in earlier eras. For example, only two generations ago, preachers widely assumed that the Bible was almost entirely patriarchal and were not aware of the impulses toward gender egalitarianism present in the Bible itself.

church that is little more than Business and Professional Women's Club, the Optimist Club, The Nature Conservancy, or the ACLU. Indeed, in the heyday of liberalism, some people viewed the church as one institution in society alongside others, whose purpose was to do its part in supporting and refining the social order. This is why so much preaching in this neighborhood leans toward the hortatory and therapeutic. Indeed, sometimes the church acts as if the rent it pays to the modern worldview is on a lease-to-buy basis with the result that the church moves almost entirely into the house of modernity.

# Gated Community

The classical postliberal response[51] to modernism is to view the church as a gated community of sorts. A gated community, in common parlance, is a neighborhood with limited access to those who do not live and own property in the neighborhood. The neighborhood may or may not literally be enclosed by some kind of fence, but vehicle and pedestrian entrance is controlled for the sake of the security and social cohesion of the residents. The insulated character of the community does not mean that those who live in the neighborhood have no concern for or interaction with the world beyond its walls, but that the line between residents and others in the world is drawn sharply.

## Characteristics of the Theological Neighborhood

Whereas evangelicals seek to convert culture to Christian theology and morality and liberals seek to accommodate Christian theology to

---

51. As with evangelical and liberals, there are a number of nuanced variations within postliberal thinking that are beyond the scope of our work. Our goal in describing a postliberal orientation toward culture in the broad strokes we use is to set up clear contrasts for the proposal we will make in the following chapter, not to assert all postliberal individuals and communities are monolithic. (For one description of the differences among postliberal and neoliberal theologians, see George Hunsinger, "Postliberal Theology," in *The Cambridge Companion to Postmodern Theology*, ed. Kevin Vanhoozer [Cambridge: Cambridge University Press, 2003], 42–45.)

cultural epistemology while they, at the same time, strive to transform culture in relation to a Christian ethical worldview, postliberals claim that the church is a culture unto itself. As with all cultures, they say, the church is a sociolinguistic construct. This epistemological stance is significantly different than that held by evangelicals and liberals. Responding to the Enlightenment concern that all knowledge be grounded on a foundation of certainty or set of first principles, both evangelical and liberal neighborhoods strive to base their faith, theology, and practices on a foundation behind scripture that is objectively real, on a foundation that is external to their finite and potentially flawed constructs of the world. For classical evangelicals, this foundation is assumed to be the history of God active in the world behind the Bible, which speaks of that history infallibly.[52] For classical liberals, this foundation is universal human experience. Against such concerns about the Christian faith corresponding with reality, postliberal thinkers begin not with a foundation lying underneath the Bible, but with the language and stories of the Bible and Christian tradition as creating reality. Instead of being concerned with whether or how Christian language and narratives appropriately *refer* to an external reality, they view these as *creating* the linguistic-social culture of the church.

This stance means that postliberals, influenced by the neo-orthodoxy of *Karl Barth*, especially reject liberalism's attempt to reconcile the Christian faith to modernity. Neither supposedly objective reason nor modern experience should have any authority over determining what the church considers to be true or how the church acts in the world. Ultimately this means that postliberals are not, in the end, concerned about the refer-

---

52. It is, again, important to note the use of the modifier *classical* with reference to evangelicalism and liberalism, especially since the lines between these schools and postliberalism are much blurrier today than our ideal descriptions suggest. For example, in an intriguing development, some evangelicals are finding postliberalism to be inviting of holding on to some of their conservative stances while, at the same time, striving to engage postmodernity; e.g., Stanley J. Grenz and John R. Franke, *Beyond Foundationalism: Shaping Theology in a Postmodern Context* (Louisville: Westminster John Knox, 2001).

ential nature of the language used by the church but with the power of that language to construct a shared reality and identity for its adherents. The narrative(s) of the faith comprise the church's own unique language that cannot be translated into "public theology," that is, theology that both (1) seeks to transform the public world beyond the church and (2) is itself evaluated by criteria that come from the larger public sphere.

The two figures most identified as founders of this school of thought are *Hans Frei* and *George Lindbeck*, who both taught at Yale. Frei is not concerned with whether the "realistic narrative" of the Bible is historically grounded but only whether it is history-like.[53] For example, he is not concerned whether the story of the resurrection is true in some historical, scientific sense but whether it is verisimilar in the sense of constructing the identity of Jesus Christ in terms of his living presence. The claim of the accounts of the resurrection "is that, in the instance of this singular individual, his identity and its manifestation involve his actual living presences. Who and what he was, did, and underwent are all inseparable from the fact that he is."[54]

Similarly, Lindbeck refutes attempts by "propositionalists" who attempt to correlate doctrine and fact and "experiential-expressivists" who interpret doctrines as symbolic of feelings and existential orientations. Instead, he speaks of doctrine as being true in a "regulative" sense, that is, in describing the rules of discourse (theological grammar) and practices within the community of faith.[55] For example, the claim that "Christ is Lord" is performatively true only as part of "a total pattern of speaking,

---

53. See Frei's two major works, *The Eclipse of the Biblical Narrative: A Study in Eighteenth and Nineteenth Century Hermeneutics* (New Haven: Yale University Press, 1974) and *The Identity of Jesus Christ: The Hermeneutical Bases of Dogmatic Theology* (Philadelphia: Fortress, 1975).

54. Frei, *Identity of Jesus Christ*, 147.

55. See Lindbeck's seminal work, *The Nature of Doctrine: Religion and Theology in a Postliberal Age* (Philadelphia: Westminster, 1984).

thinking, feeling, and acting" and is false as a crusader's battle cry "when used to authorize cleaving the skull of the infidel."[56]

Because postliberals refuse to grant the world and its criteria of reason and experience any authority over the church's self-regulating truth claims, it has no concern for apologetics. Indeed, from this perspective, using non-Christian categories of knowledge, thinking, and values of the contemporary culture to explain and defend Christian faith necessarily results in a corruption of the faith. It is not worried with defending a literal view of a six-day creation over the Big Bang theory and evolution or in interpreting the biblical creation story for its "real" meaning in light of accepting the Big Bang theory and evolution as explanations for the origin of the universe. Instead, postliberals "insist on the irreducible importance of [the biblical] stories which convey truth and preserve communal identity in a way that gets lost if we try to find what they really mean and then discard the stories."[57] This does not mean that postliberal preachers simply stand in the pulpit, read the story, and then sit down without interpreting the text for the listeners. Postliberal preachers sometimes make analogies between the ancient text and contemporary life, but the biblical story stands on its own without apologizing for its ancient character or worldview. The preacher seeks to shape the contemporary community by helping the community envision itself as being grafted into the biblical story as "our" story. In the end, the goal is that the story interpret and shape our experience of the world more than we interpret the story in light of our experience in the world. As Paul Minear, who arrived at Yale before Frei and Lindbeck and might be seen as a precursor to elements of their work, once said in response to Rudolf Bultmann, "The major difference between us, Mr. Bultmann, is clear. Your concern is that we demythologize the New Testament. Mine is that

---

56. Lindbeck, *Nature of Doctrine*, 64.

57. William C. Placher, "Postliberal Theology," in *The Modern Theologians*, David E. Ford, 2nd ed. (Oxford: Blackwell, 1997), 345.

we allow the New Testament to demythologize us."[58] So a postliberal sermon on Genesis 1 might sound much like an evangelical or liberal sermon, with the preacher drawing an analogy between God's bringing order out of chaos in the creation story with God doing the same for us today.[59] The hermeneutical orientation behind the analogy is radically different, however:

- The evangelical preacher can draw the analogy because the creation story is scientifically, historically true and speaks to the eternal character and working of God.

- The liberal preacher must draw the analogy because the creation is not literally true and, thus, requires a symbolic, metaphorical, experiential interpretation to be meaningful to modern hearers.

- The postliberal preacher can draw the analogy because the story is the church's realistic story that serves to interpret the church's identity, faith, and practices.

Postliberals, therefore, are primarily concerned with insider-speak as opposed to convincing outsiders of the trustworthiness of the faith. This does not mean, of course, that postliberals have no concern for evangelism, but it does mean that their approach to evangelism is in no way apologetic. No defense of the plausibility of the church's stories. No adapting the interpretation of the church's stories to demonstrate their meaningfulness. Simply tell the story and invite outsiders into it

58. Ron remembers J. Louis Martyn recounting this exchange in a lecture in a class at Union Theological Seminary in New York in the early 1970s.

59. For example, William H. Willimon published a sermon in the November 2001 issue of *Sojourners* after 9/11 that draws an analogy between the story of God creating order out of chaos in Genesis 1 being shaped during the Babylonian exile and America's feeling of being in a "formless void" after the terrorist attack and needing to claim that same confidence in God; see "Let There Be Light," http://sojo.net/magazine/2001/11/let-there-be-light.

that they might become insiders.[60] In other words, postliberals are concerned with maintaining the integrity of the witness of the church over the world; and when in the church's process of telling its stories to itself outsiders are attracted to the stories, they are welcomed inside the gate.

The concern to maintain the integrity of the church's witness over the world influences a postliberal approach to ethics, as well. Certainly, postliberals journey through the world, buy groceries in the world, get aid from doctors whose practice is shaped by evolutionary biology in the world, and vote in political elections. Certainly, they care about the state of the world and desire it to be a place of justice and peace. But they reside in a church neighborhood that takes an explicit countercultural stance against the world. *Stanley Hauerwas*,[61] one of the most well-known of voices that speak from a postliberal orientation, rejects the view that the church is called to engage in political action in which power is used to transform society.[62] Such an approach, he argues, is based more in a liberal philosophical orientation that values toleration, pluralism, and individual autonomy when the church "is devoted to a particular God and a particular way of life that follows Jesus Christ."[63] In other words, the church's ethical stances are rooted in an identity formed by the biblical narratives, so that the most ethical thing the church can do is to simply be the church. Hauerwas's ethics, therefore, are less concerned with principles defining the "right" action to take when faced with a specific ethical dilemma and more concerned with virtues indi-

---

60. See William H. Willimon and Stanley Hauerwas, *Preaching to Strangers: Evangelism in Today's World* (Philadelphia: Westminster John Knox, 1992); and Willimon, *The Intrusive Word: Preaching to the Baptized* (Grand Rapids: William B. Eerdmans, 1994); this work is meant as a contrast to the insider community approach to postliberal preaching as presented in Willimon's *Peculiar Speech: Preaching to the Baptized* (Grand Rapids: William B. Eerdmans, 1992).

61. The following description of Hauerwas's overarching viewpoint is drawn from William Werpehowski, "Theological Ethics," in *The Modern Theologians: An Introduction to Christian Theology in the Twentieth Century* (Malden, MA: Blackwell, 1997), 320–22.

62. Thus Hauerwas rejects H. Richard Niebuhr's highly influential view of "Christ the Transformer of Culture" in *Christ and Culture* (New York: Harper and Row, 1951).

63. Werpehowski, "Theological Ethics," 320.

vidual Christians and the community of faith as a whole should hold to live out the identity prescribed by the gospel.[64]

## *Apologetics in the Postliberal Pulpit*

While Hauerwas has an interest in preaching,[65] the best known preacher in the postliberal neighborhood is *William H. Willimon*, long-time dean of Duke University Chapel and recently retired United Methodist bishop.[66] As noted earlier, he coauthored the popular *Resident Aliens* with Hauerwas. Recent works on Barth and preaching show post-liberalism's dependence on Barth extending into the pulpit.[67] Perhaps his most important work for our purposes is *Peculiar Speech: Preaching to the Baptized*, which was published three years after he coauthored *Resident Aliens* with Hauerwas, and in which he explicitly applies the ideas of that book to the task of preaching.[68]

In this work, Willimon argues that modern preachers too often try to answer the questions of culture and deal with the human condition or common human experience in some didactic manner. Instead, we should take a "Christ against culture" stance, operating within a domain of distinctive Christian discourse that creates a distinctive Christian

---

64. See Hauerwas, *A Community of Character: Toward a Constructive Christian Social Ethic* (Notre Dame, IN: University of Notre Dame Press, 1991); and John Berkman and Michael Cartwright, eds., *The Hauerwas Reader* (Durham, NC: Duke University Press, 2001).

65. Stanley Hauerwas, *Preaching to Strangers* (Louisville: Westminster John Knox, 1992); *Disrupting Time: Sermons, Prayers, and Sundries* (Eugene, OR: Cascade, 2004); *A Cross-Shattered Church: Reclaiming the Theological Heart of Preaching* (Grand Rapids: Brazos, 2009); *Without Apology: Sermons for Christ's Church* (New York: Seabury, 2013).

66. For a good survey of his sermons, see William H. Willimon, *The Collected Sermons of William H. Willimon* (Louisville: Westminster John Knox, 2010); for an appreciative overview of his homiletic, see Michael Turner and William F. Malambri, III, eds., *A Peculiar Prophet: William H. Willimon and the Art of Preaching* (Nashville: Abingdon Press, 2004).

67. William H. Willimon, *Conversation with Barth on Preaching* (Nashville: Abingdon Press, 2006); Karl Barth and William H. Willimon, *The Early Preaching of Karl Barth: Fourteen Sermons with Commentary by William H. Willimon* (Louisville: Westminster John Knox, 2009).

68. *Peculiar Speech* (Grand Rapids: William B. Eerdmans, 1992).

community and distinctive Christian identity.[69] Thus, he rejects a hermeneutic focused on translating the biblical story into contemporary idiom so that hearers might understand it and reconcile it with contemporary knowledge. Preaching is for the baptized or for the purpose of moving hearers to be baptized. In other words, preaching is ecclesial in nature, peculiar speech for this particular community. As he names this position in a later essay,

> Our problem as preachers is not that we must render strange biblical stories intelligible to modern people but rather that these biblical stories render a strange God. If our speech doesn't move uninformed people outside the church toward baptism, or at least move jaded, tired, unformed people inside the church to a renewal of their baptism, our talk is not evangelical. Apologetics is what we do when we don't want to risk being transformed.[70]

The biblical text, for Willimon, then, is never to be submitted to the standards of contemporary epistemology (classical liberalism) but neither is his concern that the biblical text subdue contemporary epistemology (classical evangelicalism). Through preaching, listeners are invited to claim the biblical *story* as "our" story by submitting to it and allowing it to dismantle us and transform our identity as a baptized people. Since the Christian faith is a linguistic construct, preaching serves to construct the listener in line with the Christian faith, and is not in the least concerned with reconciling this construct with the construct of modern, Enlightenment knowledge or values.

Being the masterful preacher that he is, Willimon's sermons are filled with references to imagery from contemporary life. But whereas Craddock, say, uses such images to offer hearers an experience of the ancient gospel in today's world, Willimon uses such imagery from today to help

---

69. As with Hauerwas, Willimon rejects Niebuhr's option for "Christ the Transformer of Culture."

70. Willimon, "Easter Preaching as Peculiar Speech," *Journal for Preachers,* 17, no. 3 (January 1, 1994): 3.

the community enter the world created by the ancient narrative. Preaching is all about telling the church's story found in scripture and tradition in order to forge the church's identity, values, beliefs, and practices in light of the story.

We can see this clearly in a sermon on the resurrection by Willimon. Preached at Duke Chapel in 1999, "Easter as an Earthquake" focuses on Matthew 28:1-10, especially picking up on Matthew's image of the earthquake accompanying the rolling back of the stone at the empty tomb as a metaphor for radical change effected by the resurrection.[71]

Interestingly, though, Willimon begins with the image in the Gospel of John in which the disciples see the empty tomb and then simply go back home. He immediately makes a connection with Luke's version of the disciples heading back to Emmaus, refusing to cancel lunch reservations even with news of resurrection. An evangelical will move between texts in this manner to harmonize the Gospel accounts to reconstruct the historical picture behind the Gospels. A liberal trained in historical and literary criticisms would likely highlight the differences between the stories to get at the particular theology or experience the author wanted to convey to the reader. Willimon's approach, in contrast, demonstrates the postliberal sense that the New Testament canon tells *a* story of Jesus Christ that is not to be defended or picked apart. It is simply to be told and claimed.

After this small collage highlighting the stupidity of the disciples, Willimon starts turning toward the contemporary congregation by referring to Marcus Borg, a leader of the Jesus Seminar. Willimon remembers that Borg accounts for the resurrection by saying that the disciples had an experience of remembering what it was like to be with Jesus. "Just thinking about it makes him seem almost still here. Yep, by God, he *is*

---

71. Willimon *The Collected Sermons of William H. Willimon*, 195–98.

still here. Let's all close our eyes and believe real hard that he's still here. Okay?"[72] After chiding Borg and his companions in the Jesus Seminar in that vein, Willimon recalls other ways of dealing with the notion of Jesus coming back from the dead: "We modern types try to 'explain' the resurrection. One says that Jesus was in a deep, drugged coma and woke up. Another said that the disciples got all worked up in their grief and just fantasized the whole thing. But you can't 'explain' a resurrection. *Resurrection explains us.*"[73]

This perspective is a prime example of a postliberal homiletic at work. What Willimon does explicitly with this move is set up an identification between the dumb disciples and the hearers (dumb us). He grafts hearers into the story. Like the first disciples, "we" don't really understand the radical nature of Jesus's resurrection.

But along with setting up this identification, he does several other things. First, he takes a jab at a modernist, historical-critical approach to resurrection. Indeed, throughout the sermon, Willimon resists any temptation to explain or defend the resurrection or faith in it. He simply tells the story and lets it stand on its own. It is not our role to interpret the biblical story but to let it interpret us.

Second, by using language of "the same old world," Willimon hints at the idea of Christian faith as a counter cultural encounter with the world. The postliberal neighborhood is gated not to withdraw from the world but to stand over against it. Note how this theme becomes pronounced at the end of the sermon:

> God took the cruel cross and made it the means of triumph. . . . God took the worst we do—all our death-dealing doing—and led them out toward life. And the earth shook.
> A new world was thereby offered. . . .

---

72. Ibid., 195–96.

73. Ibid.

The angel plopped himself down on the stone in one final act of impudent defiance of death, and the soldiers, and all that, and said to the women, "*Don't be afraid.* You're looking for Jesus? He isn't here."

Then that angel turned to the soldiers and said, "*Be* afraid. Everything which your world is built on is being shaken."[74]

In the end, the church stands against the world because the biblical story does so.

Finally, the original passage we are considering speaks of "us" in a way that names not individual hearers sitting in the pew so much as the church as a corporate identity. This is quite subtle but reinforced with references to the church later in the sermon. The idea that the resurrection is for the church is explicit, however, in another Easter sermon Willimon preached in 2007.[75] This sermon is titled, "To Galilee," and reflects on the young man's instructions to the women at the empty tomb to tell the disciples that Jesus is going ahead of them into Galilee. "Why Galilee?" Willimon asks. The answer is, "Nobody special lived in Galilee, nobody except the *followers of Jesus. Us.*"[76] A little later in the sermon, Willimon makes absolutely clear that the "us" is the church:

> It would have been news enough that Christ rose from the dead, but the good news was that he rose *for us.* . . .
>
> If it was difficult to believe that Jesus was raised from the dead, it must have been almost impossible to believe that he was raised and returned *to us.* The result of Easter, the product of the resurrection of Christ is the church—a community of people with nothing more to convene us than the risen Christ came back to us. That's our only claim, our only hope. He came back to Galilee. He came back to us.[77]

In sum, Willimon tries neither to defend belief in the resurrection over a modernist, scientific worldview nor to translate the meaning of

---

74. Ibid., 197–98.

75. Ibid., 248–52.

76. Ibid., 249.

77. Ibid., 250.

the ancient story into something meaningful in a modern, scientific culture. He simply assumes the story has meaning, tells it, and interprets it. People in the pew would likely not catch the postliberal nuances we describe above, but that would be fine with Willimon. His goal is not to create postliberal theologians but to form the identity, faith, and practices of the church in accordance with the scripture and tradition of the church against attempts by the world to shape the church's identity, mission, theology, and behavior.

## Critical Reflection on Postliberal Preaching and Apologetics

The gated community of postliberal theology and homiletics has much to commend itself to the preacher. It is an important corrective to the evangelical and liberal neighborhoods in which an other (secular epistemology or experience) defines the terms of what is plausibly proclaimed. There is something quite appealing about simply proclaiming the faith on its own terms in contrast to defending it against outside authorities or allowing it to be subsumed by terms defined by others in modernity.

But this stance is not without its problems. First, to isolate the Christian story from *any* critique from outside the faith is to assume that scripture and tradition are the sole authorities for making meaning in a Christian manner. Surely reason and experience have a place in the Christian faith, even if we reassert the primacy of scripture and tradition. One particularly troubling example is that the postliberal position does not have a natural venue for the experiences of the marginalized, including those who have been marginalized *by the church*, to serve as a critique of the Christian story. Postliberals would certainly allow for such critique to be applied to, say, the patriarchal *use* of the biblical text; but it does not invite a critique of the patriarchal nature of the biblical text itself.

Second, the claim that the Christian story should stand on its own instead of engaging apologetically with culture is not following the model actually found in scripture and tradition which postliberals claim as the authority for our practices. Paul employed Greek philosophical concepts and images in his letters. One purpose behind the Gospels was to defend the church as a proper heir of Israel's traditions against claims that this was not so. Nearly every line of the Apostles' Creed, as a baptismal profession of faith, was developed to counter Gnostic claims that challenged traditional (historical) understandings of the church's faith. It could (and should) be argued that apologetical engagement with the world is part and parcel of Christian identity and a foundational Christian practice.

Another aspect of the postliberal orientation that is appealing is the view that scripture interprets us instead of us interpreting scripture. The authority of scripture should reach to the level of shaping the identity of individual Christians and the church corporately. Indeed, preachers across the theological spectrum (even Bultmann!) would agree that the biblical story is our story; we are grafted into it in a way that it names who we are and who we ought to be.

But preachers living in other neighborhoods would challenge at least two aspects of the way postliberals make this assertion. First, most would refuse to make the claim in an either/or fashion in which scripture interpreting us is placed against our interpreting scripture. Instead, they would say, we interpret scripture critically using modern and postmodern hermeneutical lenses *so that* it interprets us modern and postmodern Christians.

Second, while postliberals recognize the Christian faith is a construct among many constructs in the world and, thus, admit that the church's interpretation of the world is a subjective one, they do not seem to recognize that their *reading* the narrative of the Christian faith inside the

53

church is also a subjective, ideologically influenced activity that is self-serving, in the sense that it promotes their own social power. In truth, there is no way to let the story speak for itself completely. Reader-oriented hermeneutics have taught us that reading is not simply discovering meaning, it is a process of *making* meaning. To read a text *is* to interpret it. So while postliberals may think they are allowing the text more of an autonomous voice than liberals (or evangelicals) do, in truth they are first interpreting the text through contemporary hermeneutical lenses (for example, realistic history or sociolinguistic culture) that come from outside of scripture *before* scripture, in turn, interprets them/us.

Finally, perhaps the most appealing aspect of the postliberal neighborhood, and one that is the foundation for the two just discussed, is the honest recognition that the Christian faith is a sociolinguistic construct. More than any other aspect of this neighborhood's orientation, this one puts the *post* in postliberal. Indeed, postliberalism is a significant move toward postmodernity in that it rejects the idea that reason is objective and avoids the search for a universal foundation for knowledge. This allows postliberal preachers to speak in a traditional and often conservative-sounding manner without apology (in both senses of the word)—without having to assume the language refers to the same reality that traditionalists and conservatives would claim it refers to. The language of the faith constructs reality instead of simply describing reality.

But this concept is also problematic in a number of ways. These problems do not counter the recognition that Christianity is a construct, but the way postliberals interpret and live out the sense of the faith being a construct. First, the postliberal orientation, when pushed where its logic fully leads, has no need for the construct of the Christian faith to refer to any reality outside itself. Willimon himself has backed away from this aspect in recent times in the sense that the proliferation of works on Christian practices do not seem connected to the really real God. As he asks of one author, "Is this god whom you are following [by doing these practices] actually God or not?"[78] For Willimon, "God" is not simply a sociolinguistic construct. The church's faith, identity, and practices must indeed have an external reference that guides the church, as sure as a compass, helps someone find their way while traveling in many directions because it always points north.

Another problem with postliberalism that shows it is not as postmodern as some claim is that in recognizing Christian faith and the church as a sociolinguistic construct, it devalues pluralism. Postliberals do not withdraw completely from the world, but they do insulate the faith from any critique in that they see no value in engaging other constructs as having the possibility of offering the church something worth considering as part of its faith, identity, and practices. Is Willimon's "actual God" so small that only the Christian construct is worth considering?

A final problem with the way postliberals emphasize the church as a sociolinguistic construct is the naïveté of assuming (or aiming for) the idea that individual Christians and the Christian community is or can be constructed by the Christian story/traditions alone. Human identity is shaped by a *matrix* of sociolinguistic cultures all at the same time. We are creatures of a multiplicity of culturally-constructed values, identities, and practices. The pews are filled with people who have been shaped and continue to be shaped by various versions of sexual, gender, economic, educational, political, religious, geographical, ethnic, racial, familial, ideological, generational, technological, entertainment, journalistic cultures and subcultures. To try to preach in such a way that only the Christian cultural construct takes hold in a listener is not only naïve, it goes against human nature. It is legitimate to suggest that the Christian story and

---

78. William H. Willimon, "Too Much Practice: Second Thoughts on a Theological Movement," *Christian Century* 127, no. 5 (March 9, 2010): 22–25.

traditions hold the primary place in shaping Christians' individual and shared worldviews and behaviors, but there are no gates strong enough (nor should there be) to isolate the faith and those who hold it from all of the other influences on the human species.

# Conclusion

The evangelical Hatfield-McCoy feud, the liberal apartment dwelling, and the postliberal gated community are three distinct approaches to dealing with modernism. The first two live in different apologetic postures while the third rejects apologetics. Each position has strengths that make them worthy of consideration for homiletical strategies. But in our estimation, all three have problems of such magnitude that they will not serve the preacher well in postmodernity. Postmodernity calls for neither an apologetic nor an unapologetic approach to preaching but for a postapologetic approach. We visit that neighborhood in the following chapters.

# Chapter 2

# A Postapologetic
# Neighborhood

I n each of the neighborhoods we have visited so far, the characteristics of life are quite different. The Hatfields and McCoys regard
one another with suspicion and keep rifles loaded to protect their
turf. In an apartment complex, the owner sets the rules for the building
and the residents pay rent. A tenant's association may negotiate with the
owner, but the owner still has ultimate control of the building. A gated
community exists to preserve the sameness of quality of life in the neighborhood. The guard controls who comes in and who goes out.

In the best multicultural neighborhoods, people from different
cultures live alongside one another in mutuality: African Americans,
Latina/Latinos, Asians, Native Americans, Pacific Islanders, and people of European origin, not to mention people of different sexual orientations, different economic classes, different political commitments,
different religions, indeed, as many forms of difference as there are
people. Within these larger communities, people differ—Japanese,
Chinese, and Koreans all originate from Asia, but their worlds can be
quite distinct. When people in the neighborhood interact with others
in a context of respect, residents learn to understand the world from

one another's perspectives and to adapt some of their values, customs, and practices in light of what they discover in others. A recent immigrant from Kenya may engage elements of North American culture through a Kenyan worldview, but a third generation Kenyan-American may identify much more with North American culture while holding on to traditional elements of their ethnic heritage. As people of Eurocentric origin, for instance, both Wes and Ron grew up on fried chicken, mashed potatoes and cream gravy, sweet tea, and deep-dish black raspberry cobbler. But we now also love greens, frijoles, and kimchi, sometimes on the same dinner table.[1]

The multicultural neighborhood and what happens in it is a good metaphorical matrix for the postmodern world and for postapologetic preaching in that neighborhood.[2] Recognizing and honoring diversity is a hallmark of postmodernism. The postapologetic preacher, like a good neighbor in a multicultural setting, enters into conversation with others in the neighborhood—listening, questioning, offering perspectives, being willing to change, being willing to challenge, and the multitude of other dynamics that are part of genuine conversations. Whereas classical evangelicals feud with culture, liberals accommodate to culture, and postliberals stand against culture, postapologetic preachers enter into deep give-and-take conversation with culture. If we distinguish the different schools of thought in terms of the flow of influence desired by preachers in the different camps, the following table shows what is at stake in the differences:

---

1. Both Wes and Ron grew up in relatively evangelical circles but made the move to the liberal neighborhood as conscious choices in college. Our formative theological thinking took place in the liberal tradition. While we are critical of aspects of both the evangelical and liberal approaches, we are also deeply grateful to both. In ways different to each of us, we still manifest characteristics of each, especially the liberal side.

2. For heuristic purpose, we present positive dimensions of multicultural neighborhoods. Diversity can also become the occasion of conflict among the different groups. Problems arise not from diversity itself but from the ways in which some individuals and groups respond to others and from the ways in which others sometimes present themselves.

| |
|---|
| Evangelical |
| faith ——→ culture |
| Liberal |
| faith ←—— culture |
| Postliberal |
| faith ‖ culture |
| Postapologetic |
| faith ←—→ culture |

Having drawn the lines between the postapologetic neighborhood and the others as boldly as we have for heuristic purposes, we must now step back and note that there are certainly voices in each of the other three neighborhoods that do have aspects of give-and-take conversation with culture in ways similar to the postapologetic stance. To introduce our explication of postapologetics, then, this chapter first reviews some evangelical (and post-evangelical) and postliberal figures who move in the direction of becoming more conversational with the diverse voices that constitute postmodern culture and then names how the work of some liberals especially have helped create the environment for a conversational approach to preaching. The heart of the chapter is an exploration of postapologetic conversation as an appropriate mode of relationship with culture that can both participate in God's purposes and be at home in postmodernity.

## Conversational Traffic Patterns Merging into Postapologetics

Although neighborhoods often exist for decades, they do not remain static. Change results from any number of factors: evolving dreams and desires of the residents, natural process of growth and decay, the weather, fears, aging, new possibilities afforded by technology, or by moving to other areas. Giant trees die and are replaced by seedlings. Streets are resurfaced, rerouted, and even renamed. Tile sewers from the 1920s crumble and are replaced by PVC lines. The young couples just out of college in the 1950s filled the yards and streets with children who, over the decades, grew up and made their way to the suburbs while the population of the old neighborhood aged until younger families again move in, refurbish the houses, and fill the yards and streets with (fewer) children. Property values rise and fall and rise again. Old technology gives way to new. One racial or ethnic group may have been the first to live in a neighborhood, but over time the population shifted to another group and then into a truly multicultural setting.

The same is true in theological and homiletical neighborhoods. In the previous chapter we looked at the street maps of "classical" evangelical, liberal, and postliberal neighborhoods. But, of course, these neighborhoods have changed and continue to change. Over the past thirty years, some of their residents have begun to adapt to emerging postmodernity. *Many of these adaptations move in the direction of conversational approaches to theology and preaching.* They not only clearly recognize the presence of the other, but consider ways that engagement with the other might enlarge or reshape their theological and homiletical points of view while being in continuity with their basic theological commitments. Most changes, however, stop short of the fully conversational approach we have in mind. In the following material, we have space to consider only representative examples.

## Evangelical Commute toward Conversation

Whereas classical evangelicalism and the modern world often related to one another much like the Hatfields and the McCoys, many third generation evangelicals are less polarized and more reciprocal, more conversational. We discuss a few representative examples.

*John Stackhouse* acknowledges the radical relativism and pluralism of the world in which we live and calls for a "humble apologetics" that does not seek to establish absolute truth, but wants to help people develop confidence in the *plausibility* of Christian faith. Rather than evidence or proof, humble apologists speak of grounds, warrants, or justifications for belief.[3] Ultimately, Stackhouse contends that the church should engage in apologetics "because they want their neighbors to take Christianity more seriously than they otherwise might," and that Christians might "decide to follow Jesus Christ or to follow [Christ] more closely, as a result of such conversations."[4] Whether focusing on conversation inside the church or on the church's conversation with outsiders, the apologetic community listens and speaks with humility and with respect for the other. Apologetics is "an act of love," a gift which the apologist offers the recipient without trying to force the other to accept it.[5]

The humble apologist, in other words, recognizes the relativity of all perception, and wants to understand why others think, believe, and act as they do. Indeed, the beginning of apologetics is listening to the other, taking seriously the viewpoints of the other, clarifying and dealing with the most important questions (so as not to deal in caricature or to distract), and adapting the process of engaging the other to the context, especially to the modes of receptivity at work in the other.[6] Only after careful listening to the other does the apologist then shape a response in such a way as to respect the perspective of the other.

---

3. John C. Stackhouse, *Humble Apologetics: Defending the Faith Today* (New York: Oxford University Press, 2002), 90.

4. Ibid., 86.

5. Ibid., 140–41.

6. Ibid., 161–64, 167–73, 182–89, 198–203.

*Stanley Grenz* was a clear and irenic evangelical who was fully aware of the theological issues surfaced by postmodernism. His descriptions of postmodernism do what every good participant in a conversation should do: he avoids caricature and articulates the perspective of the other with respect, clarity, and nuance.[7] In his *Renewing the Center: Evangelical Theology in the Post-Theological Era,* Grenz offers a crisp review of the history of evangelical theology, taking into account its apologetic origin and development. With a touch of humor, Grenz summarizes:

> Despite the seemingly bewildering plethora of options currently touted [regarding evangelical responses to postmodernism], the most widely heralded submissions boil down to a few simple alternatives. We are told that as evangelicals we should either batten down the hatches and wait for the storm to pass, ignore postmodernism as a passing fad that will soon give way to "post-postmodernism," launch a philosophical jihad with the goal of stamping out postmodernism and thereby make the world safe for Christian faith, or do an end run around both postmodernism and modernism by resurrecting some idyllic premodern era.[8]

In contrast, Grenz calls for "an apologetic theology appropriate to the emerging postmodern (and perhaps post-theological) context."[9] This apologetic puts together a "belief mosaic" made up of different pieces whose cumulative effect is to make belief a rational possibility. This apologetic theological approach centers in conversation. Grenz states that "theological construction—the attempt to delineate what ought to be

---

7. We think especially of *A Primer on Postmodernism* (Grand Rapids: William B. Eerdmans, 1996). The qualities we describe here pervade Grenz's many other works dealing with evangelical theology in the emerging postmodern context, for example, *Revisioning Evangelical Theology* (Downers Grove: IVP, 1993); *Theology for the Community of God* (Grand Rapids: William B. Eerdmans, 2000, o.p. 1994); *What Christians Really Believe . . . and Why* (Louisville: Westminster John Knox, 1998); and with John R. Franke, *Beyond Foundationalism: Shaping Theology in a Postmodern Context* (Louisville: Westminster John Knox, 2000). Grenz, of course, is only one evangelical author who moves in this broadening stream, but his work is a particularly good point of entry into this discussion not only because of its own clarity but because of the number of additional theologians with whom he interacts.

8. Stanley J. Grenz, *Renewing the Center: Evangelical Theology in a Post-Theological Era* (Grand Rapids: Baker Academic, 2000), 21–22.

9. Ibid., 19.

the belief-mosaic of the Christian Church—may be characterized as an ongoing conversation that the participants in the faith community share as to the meaning of the cultural symbols through which Christians express their understanding of the world they inhabit."[10]

The goal of the conversation is to indicate "the value of the Christian worldview for illumining human experience, as well as our human understanding of our world." Grenz underscores, "In this manner, evangelical theology retains the apologetic focus that has characterized it since the 1940s."[11]

For Grenz, this conversation brings together three resources. The first is the Bible framed in a trinitarian context, and with sensitivity to legitimate possibilities of interpretation. The second is the Spirit at work fashioning a community. The Spirit and the community exist in reciprocal relationship: the Spirit speaks through community and the community speaks the word of the Spirit (community includes tradition). The third resource is the Spirit moving through the particularities of the cultural context.[12] "The ultimate authority in the church is the Spirit speaking through Scripture"; however, this discourse is always particular to the context in which it takes place.[13] To come to as clear an understanding as possible of the Spirit's speaking, the church engages in conversation with these sources. True to his evangelical orientation, however, Grenz limits the way he views the Spirit speaking in contemporary contexts:

> Whatever [genuine] speaking [of the Spirit] that occurs through other media does not come as a speaking against the [biblical] text. To pit the Spirit's voice in culture against the Spirit speaking through scripture would be to fall prey to the foundationalist trap. It would require that

10. Ibid., 206–9.

11. Ibid., 205.

12. Ibid., 209.

13. Ibid.

we elevate some dimension of contemporary thought or experience as a human universal that forms the criterion for determining what in the Bible is or is not acceptable.[14]

In their similar but differing ways, Grenz and Stackhouse are moving toward the kind of conversational approach we propose. For Grenz, the community listens to scripture, the Spirit, and the context so as to be open to the possibility of the church changing aspects of its perception. Traffic does flow two ways on the apologetic street—from the Bible/Spirit to the culture and the interpreting community and back. For Grenz, the traffic travels largely in Christian neighborhoods with forays into other neighborhoods. For Stackhouse, the traffic is more metropolitan, but still largely takes place under the guidance of a Christian driver's manual: the breadth and transformative power of the conversation is still restrained in that it begins and is delimited by basic Christian convictions, especially the doctrine of the Trinity.

From the evangelical neighborhood also come some writers related to the Emergent Church movement, who are sometimes called post-evangelicals. They drive even closer to conversational neighborhoods than Stackhouse or Grenz, but take many different routes to get there. John S. McClure calls them "consummate theological pragmatists—cherry-picking just about everyone (Orthodox, Taize, Roman Catholic, postliberals, liberals, etc.). Their passion is for mission, that is, following in Jesus's footsteps today."[15]

*Brian McLaren* is one of the most influential of the post-evangelicals.[16] His conversational viewpoint is captured in the title of one of his widely read books, *A Generous Orthodoxy.* He writes in response to the breakdown of the modern viewpoint and to the polarization of

14. Ibid., 210.

15. John S. McClure, personal correspondence with Ron Allen, February 22, 2014.

16. Doug Pagitt, who is discussed in the next chapter, is also representative of the post-evangelicals.

the liberal and evangelical camps.[17] McLaren leaves behind the modern ideas that we can attain the pure, certain, objective, foundational, and universal knowledge, and embraces postmodern notions, especially the ideas that our knowledge is always partial, diverse, conditioned, and is often self-serving.

Similar to Stackhouse's phrase "humble apologetics," McLaren's "generous orthodoxy" represents an intentional and significant tension. In terms of "orthodoxy," McLaren sees himself in the mainstream of evangelical, Christian tradition. Yet, the description *generous* indicates that the attitude toward others, especially with different viewpoints, is more open to others than is often the case in the evangelical neighborhood. Generous orthodoxy is more concerned with Christian practice centered in Jesus than in correct and comprehensive doctrinal statements. While McLaren does not use the language of apologetics a great deal, his enterprise is apologetic in character in that he writes for a range of people, including those "who may not be Christian and wondering why anyone would want to be," Christians who are "struggling, questioning, and looking for reasons to stay in," and even those who "have officially left the Christian community" but realize they have left part of their heart and wonder if they might someday return.[18] Given these audiences, preachers should not so much defend their understandings of the faith against attack as explain their beliefs and practices in relationship to other beliefs and practices.

Conversation plays a critical role in this process. McLaren writes, "I'm saying little or nothing new, but rather I'm listening to a wider variety of older and newer voices than most people do. I'm trying to take them all seriously."[19] John Franke expands,

---

17. Brian McLaren, *A Generous Orthodoxy* (Grand Rapids: Zondervan, 2004). McLaren identifies Grenz as a theological mentor: 23–24.

18. Ibid., 16.

19. Ibid., 22.

Because generous orthodoxy is aware of the need to keep listening and learning in openness to the Spirit and the world for the sake of the gospel, it seeks to keep conversations going, and not to end them. Generous orthodoxy does not so much specify a particular point or position as it establishes a spacious territory defined by certain distinct boundaries in which there is space to live, more, and breathe, while exploring the wonders and mysteries of the faith.[20]

McLaren pushes at these "distinct boundaries." On the one hand, he names in evangelical tones that generosity is limited by the faith represented in the Apostles' and Nicene Creeds, and especially by scripture, which "remains above the creeds."[21] On the other, he says in a conversational tone that orthodoxy is bounded by the limitations of our formulations, by charity toward those of other traditions "who may have understood some things better than our group," by courage to follow our own convictions (even when unpopular), and the diligence to persevere, even when we seem lost or feel discouraged.[22]

## Postliberal Commute toward Conversation

A reader might think that with its sectarian proclivity postliberalism would be averse to a conversational perspective: "We have all we need inside our gated community." Several postliberals, however, promote conversation as an important aspect of theological reflection, even if the range of conversation they propose is somewhat limited. These postliberals recognize the potential benefits of opening the gates to their neighborhood and learning things from outsiders that can improve their neighborhood. In a gated community, talk about change in the neighborhood takes place within the bounds of the protective covenant that members sign in order to live in the community. In a similar way,

---

20. John Franke, "Generous Orthodoxy in a Changing World," foreword to McLaren, *A Generous Orthodoxy*, 13–14.

21. McLaren, *A Generous Orthodoxy*, 28.

22. Ibid., 30.

conversation within the postliberal church and between the church and outsiders tends to take place within the theological commitments of the community. Moreover, such interchange can help postliberals shape how they present their culture to other cultures in witness and in seeking partnerships that different cultures can undertake together.

*William C. Placher*, one of the most eloquent and direct postliberals on the subject of conversation, sets the stage for thinking of postliberals in relationship to conversation by pointing out that Christians should "believe in the truth of their own claims." The truth at the center of Christian life is the pattern of Jesus's life. By looking at this life, Christians will see "a pattern that recurs again and again elsewhere in the Bible, in extrabiblical history, and in their own lives."[23] The efficacy of this pattern cannot be "proven" in the Enlightenment sense. The community's confidence in the pattern comes from the community's perception that the pattern explains their life as a community (as well as their own individual lives). Placher enlarges by hypothesizing what a believer might say:

> I'm not claiming this [Christian story] is just my way of looking at things. I really think this is the right way, the way that makes the most sense. Oh, of course I'm sure I have a lot of the details wrong, and on some matters those who see things very differently may be closer to the truth than I am—but I think I've got hold of something fundamentally right about the overall picture. By saying that, I mean that I believe that nothing will ever come along that renders this way of looking at things impossible, and that, indeed, someday, as the picture of things emerges more completely, the pattern I see, which I concede is at the moment tricky to catch a glimpse of, will emerge so clearly that anyone who looks will basically see things this way.[24]

---

23. William C. Placher, *Unapologetic Theology: A Christian Voice in a Pluralistic Conversation* (Louisville: Westminster John Knox, 1989), 126.

24. Ibid., 129–30.

When confronted by anomalies, Christians should admit "that these things have us mystified and constitute a problem for our vision of things."[25] Postliberal Christians believe "that at some future time this now ambiguous pattern will become clear. What we see in a mirror dimly, we will then see face-to-face."[26]

Given this larger framework, Placher raises the natural question: "Why should adherents of one tradition feel any need to talk with those who do not stand within their community?"[27] Placher's answer is similar to rationales for participating in conversation we have already mentioned. Beginning with the biblical period, communities of faith "have recognized the importance of conversation with 'outsiders' for their own life, health, and faithfulness."[28] As one would expect of a postliberal apologetic for conversation with those beyond the neighborhood, Placher begins with models found in the narratives of the Bible. All human beings are made in the image of God. Some ancient Israelites believed that the same God who liberated Israel from Egypt also brought the Arameans from Kir. Jesus pointed to Gentiles as sources of theological insight (e.g., the centurions at Capernaum and at the cross).

He proposes conversation with the other, also, based on tradition. Indeed, the history of the Christian tradition provides evidence of the value of such conversations precisely for Christianity's own faithful development: from patristic lessons learned from Plato to Aquinas's dependence on the Islamic interpreters of Aristotle, to the ways Marxists have helped Christians rediscover their call to social witness to the lessons Martin Buber taught a whole generation of Christian theologians.[29]

25. Ibid., 129.
26. Ibid., 126.
27. Ibid., 115–16.
28. Ibid., 116.
29. Ibid.

For Placher the most important reason for participating in conversations with others is that they help the Christian community enhance its own faith and practice. This is true with respect to both the internal life of the community and to its witness in the larger world. Conversation with outsiders helps the church adapt its witness to the situation of those outside the Christian orb. And, since an important postliberal conviction is that the church can make alliance with non-Christian groups when working for social justice, conversation can help identify groups with whom the church can make common cause. Moreover, Placher acknowledges that people outside the church may benefit from dialogue with the Christian community.

*Charles Campbell*, a postliberal homiletician, does not explicitly use the language of conversation a great deal, but he does employ aspects of a conversational model into practice in his approach to preaching. Campbell takes a postliberal approach to the story of Jesus as the normative pattern for Christian life.[30] Constitutive of this story is a tension between (1) this present world as a broken old age under the domination of principalities and powers, and (2) Jesus as God's agent in the dominion-free new creation. The congregation lives in a liminal situation: between the ages.[31] The old world is passing away, but the new age is not completely here. This liminality will continue until the new world is finally and fully here. Although Campbell does not describe the sermon in explicitly conversational terms, his understanding of the sermon has qualities that are associated with conversation. The sermon is a liminal space in which the preacher invites the congregation to consider the distorted, destructive aspects of the present along with the new world that God is already bringing about. Campbell uses the figure of the fool (in the Pauline

30. Charles L. Campbell, *Preaching Jesus: New Directions for Homiletics in Hans Frei's Postliberal Theology* (Grand Rapids: William B. Eerdmans, 1997).

31. Charles L. Campbell and Johan H. Cilliers, *Preaching Fools: The Gospel as a Rhetoric of Folly* (Waco: Baylor University Press, 2012), 21–23.

sense, or in the medieval sense of the fool in the community whose behavior often interrupts the life of the community in such a way as to provoke the community to look at themselves afresh) to describe the preacher and preaching. Campbell writes about the sermon in a lyrical way. The sermon

> interrupts and unsettles normative discourse in order to unmask the old age and open a space where the new creation might be perceived. Such rhetoric is unsettled and liminal, playful and creative, open—never closed. It is the opposite of iron rhetoric and iron theology and circled wagons, all of which seek stability, control, security—and usually domination. A rhetoric of folly does not operate with maxims and eternalize; it is open to others and flourishes among fragments, in the bi-vocal spaces created by paradoxes and metaphors, parody and irony. Such rhetoric resists a definition of preaching that presupposes that truth can be conveyed as a finished product or a recipe that works in a timeless way. Rather, trusting the unsettling foolishness of God, the rhetoric of folly seeks to open up liminal spaces for new perception and new life, in playful collaboration with the congregation among whom the Spirit moves to form and re-form.[32]

Like many conversations still in progress, the sermon, thus, has "a tensive, dynamic, unfinished character."[33]

Engaging others plays an important role in helping the preacher move toward the sermon. When introducing his exploration of how the principalities and the powers dominate this world and of how the work of the preacher includes encouraging resistance to the powers, Campbell says,

> I write from a position of great privilege. . . . I do not presume to speak to or for people who live on the margins of privilege and power, though I hope my reflections may be of some help in these contexts. Although I write from a position of privilege, however, this book has been shaped profoundly by voices of people who wrestle with the powers from situations of oppression. In particular, over the past few years homeless

---

32. Ibid., 216.
33. Ibid., 134–85.

people, and gay, lesbian, bisexual and transgender people have been my teachers, and have changed my life. They have helped me glimpse more fully the powers' deadly work in the world, as well as my own complicity with that work.[34]

The encounter with others helps Campbell to understand better the story itself (especially its life-shaping power), his own life and witness in relationship to that story, and the implications of the story for others. While sermon preparation takes place under the aegis of the story of Jesus, it includes listening carefully to the experience of others. Indeed, says Campbell, "We need dialogue [in order to] exist; we need to look into the eyes of others, and through the eyes of others; we actually cannot become ourselves without others."[35]

## Liberal Migration into Conversation

Some theologians who formerly lived in liberal neighborhoods have led the move into multicultural, conversational neighborhoods. Sometimes referred to as revisionists, these scholars offer perspectives that have been formative for our own journeys.[36] We discuss two representatives of this migration.

*David Tracy* has been especially influential in his use of conversation as the basis of hermeneutics.[37] Since, in the postmodern world (with its deconstructive tendencies), we have come to recognize both the plurality and ambiguity of the classic traditions and texts that have formed us, "interpretation, on the model of conversation, is a complex

34.   Charles L. Campbell, *The Word before the Powers: An Ethic of Preaching* (Louisville: Westminster John Knox, 2002), 4–5; see also Stanley Saunders and Charles L. Campbell, *The Word on the Street: Performing the Scriptures in the Urban Context* (Grand Rapids: William B. Eerdmans, 2000).

35.   Campbell and Cilliers, *Preaching Fools*, 203.

36.   For a helpful overview of the relationship of revisionist and liberal theology, see James J. Buckley, "Revisionists and Liberals," in *The Modern Theologians: An Introduction to Christian Theology in the Twentieth Century*, ed. David F. Ford, 2nd ed. (Malden, MA: Blackwell, 1997), 327–42.

37.   His work that focuses most directly on conversation is David Tracy, *Plurality and Ambiguity: Hermeneutics, Religion, Hope* (San Francisco: Harper and Row, 1987).

phenomenon comprised of three elements: text, interpreter, and their interaction grounded in questioning."[38]

His conversational hermeneutic is an expansion of Paul Tillich's hermeneutic of correlation. In Tillich's correlation model, as described in chapter 1, the preacher correlates a significant contemporary question or issue with voices in the Bible and Christian tradition. The preacher assumes that the preacher can find a perspective in the Bible or tradition (presented in ancient, symbolic terms) that provides a satisfactory resolution to the question or issue.

Tracy, in contrast, proposes a hermeneutic of *mutual critical correlation* because scripture and tradition do not always contain resources that help today's community make sense (either directly or by analogy) of contemporary experience and issues. Indeed, the Bible and the Christian tradition contain some elements that contravene how many people who live on this side of the Enlightenment understand and experience.[39] From an ethical perspective, not only has the church *used* some of the content of the Bible and Christian tradition oppressively, but some of it *is* oppressive. Mutual critical correlation maintains classic liberalism's apologetic interest in a faith that is intellectually compatible with contemporary, especially scientific, worldviews, while heightening the attention given to ethical matters, especially to multiple forms of oppression and injustice.

For the theologian of mutual critical correlation, the Bible contains both important resources for the present as well as material that distorts and even corrupts God's purposes. The preacher not only uses the resources of the Bible and the tradition to interpret (criticize) the present, but uses voices in the present to critique viewpoints in the Bible and

---

38. Ibid., 28.

39. David Tracy, *Blessed Rage for Order: The New Pluralism in Theology* (Minneapolis: Winston Seabury, 1975), 45–47, 79–81; and *The Analogical Imagination: Christian Theology and the Culture of Pluralism* (New York: Crossroad, 1981), 371–72, 405–11, 421–23.

the tradition. While the preacher gives priority to the Bible and Christian tradition in theological dialogue, the preacher does not take it for granted that particular biblical texts or traditional statements (or overarching perspectives in those traditions) represent God's emancipatory purposes. The preacher thinks critically with the congregation about what the biblical and traditional material invites its readers to believe and do. At times, the Bible and tradition will help make theological sense of the present situation. At other times, the present situation will call the Bible and tradition into question. In the latter cases, the preacher helps the congregation think about what it most deeply believes and how it can embody God's purposes as fully as possible.

*Clark Williamson* also argues that conversation is at the heart of this theological process. The community, walking its way through history, has to make sense of its faith in relation to the situation in which it finds itself and to make sense of the situation in relation to its faith. It has to revise its understanding of the tradition in order to include this new situation in it, and it has to understand this situation in the light of its faith in order to know what to do in that situation. It engages in a two-way conversation between its context and its inherited tradition with the aim of being able to answer the question, What are we, as the people of the Way, to do in this situation?[40]

For Williamson, as for Tracy, conversation is characterized by openness. The interaction between the ancient faith and contemporary context is open to multiple voices and perspectives. However, "This [approach] does not mean that a conversational theology never disagrees with another viewpoint. It means, rather, that the grounds for disagreement can be reached only after we can fairly be said to understand those

---

40. Clark M. Williamson, *Way of Blessing, Way of Life: A Christian Theology* (St. Louis: Chalice, 1999), 37. Williamson develops a comprehensive theology through conversation with the process school of theology, the writings of Paul Tillich, post-Holocaust theology, postliberal theology (narrative theology), and feminist theology.

with whom we disagree."[41] For Williamson, disagreement, or difference, is essential to conversation as an ethical element.

> A genuine conversation has its ethic. Conversation is not a form of verbal warfare in which winning (at all costs) is the goal. In authentic conversation, no party to the conversation dominates either the conversation or the other parties. The topic dominates the conversation. For example, in conversation with the scriptures, the topic or question dominates. . . . For a conversationalist, anything and anyone can be questioned. In scripture, the God of Israel can not only be questioned but approves of being questioned. That leads us to this definition of idolatry: An idol is anything or anyone that claims, implicitly or explicitly, to be above question.[42]

One purpose of the theological conversation is to generate norms that the community can use to gauge the degree to which its beliefs and practices reflect the best of its understandings of God and of God's purposes.[43] Williamson calls attention to three norms:

- Appropriateness to the community's deepest beliefs about God

- Credibility, that is, logically coherent and internally and believable from the perspective of contemporary worldview

- Moral plausibility, that is, concerned for the moral treatment of all involved, especially according to the norm of appropriateness[44]

---

41. Ibid., 4.

42. Ibid., 3–4.

43. On these norms, see ibid., 29–32, 77–82, 86–88.

44. Ron has written extensively with Williamson and has made extensive use of these norms in his approach to preaching; for example: Williamson and Allen, *A Credible and Timely Word: Process Theology and Preaching* (St. Louis: Chalice, 1991); idem., *The Teaching Minister* (Louisville: Westminster John Knox, 1991); *idem. Adventures of the Spirit: A Guide to Worship from the Perspective of Process Theology* (Lanham, MD: University Press of America, 1997). These norms also inform their three-volume commentary on the lectionary from the perspective of correcting Christian anti-Judaism: *Preaching the Gospels without Blaming the Jews: A Lectionary Commentary* (Louisville: Westminster John Knox, 2004); *Preaching the Letters without Dismissing the Law: A Lectionary Commentary* (Louisville: Westminster John Knox, 2005); and *Preaching the Old Testament: A Lectionary Commentary* (Louisville: Westminster John Knox, 2006).

While these norms give the community a place to stand in the midst of the swelling tide of postmodernism, they are themselves the subject of ongoing conversation. A preacher or community can use these norms to measure the theological and ethical perspectives of a biblical text, a statement of doctrine, a voice in history, or a contemporary proposal. However, Williamson notes they are "provisional understandings," as, indeed, "all our understandings are provisional."[45] The conversation is always going on.

## Postapologetic Conversation

Our proposal for a postapologetic, conversational approach to preaching evolves from the conversational approach to theology represented by Tracy and Williamson. As we move toward describing the dialogical content and attitude, we can juxtapose it to the definition offered in chapter 1 of classical apologetics as a theological/homiletical approach that uses the categories of knowledge, thinking, and values of the contemporary culture to explain and defend Christian faith. This is done in response to explicit or implicit misunderstanding, challenges, and attacks in order to commend that very faith to both those outside and inside the church. Our own proposal is sympathetic with this endeavor but also recognizes that traditional apologetic approaches that grew up in and were a response to modernism are not fully appropriate ways for the church to share its faith in a *postmodern* world. Therefore, we propose to adapt an apologetic posture into a *post*apologetic one.

### Post?

What constitutes the *post* in postapologetics? As some argue that postmodernism is not (should not be) a full rejection of modernism but

45. Williamson, *Way of Blessing*, 23.

a critique of elements of it and an attempt to move beyond it, so, for us, postapologetics (1) embraces the apologetic posture toward the world (in the company of evangelicals and liberals over postliberals) while (2) rejecting the power given to the culture in that posture that forces the church either into a defensive stance, which desires to conquer culture, or a subordinate stance, in which the church surrenders to culture. We recognize that the church is a distinct culture among cultures that can (and should) not simply merge with the wider culture or the church. In this broad sense, we have some common ground with postliberals and evangelicals. However, we (1) also value the fact that individual Christians and the church as a community are shaped by participation in multiple cultures and (2) intentionally seek to bring church culture into conversation with other cultures for the sake of mutual benefit.

Our postapologetic orientation draws, in part, from a postmodern appreciation of 1 Peter 3:15-16. First Peter is most likely addressed to late-first-century Gentile Christians who were being persecuted mainly in the sense of public shaming and social ostracism (1:6-7; 2:12, 20-23; 3:6, 9, 13-18; 4:1-4, 12-19; 5:8-10). Because of their Christian identity, their communal practices, and their ethical behavior that distinguished them from the broader culture with which they previously identified, they experienceed the world as "aliens" and "exiles" (or "sojourners") (1:1, 17; 2:11). The author, however, does not interpret this situation as reason for them to despise or withdraw from the world, but, instead, offers the addressees encouragement in the face of their suffering and instructs them to maintain their unique identity while engaging the world in order to offer the gospel to the world (2:11-4:6). They are to be a holy and distinct people (1:14; 2:5, 9) but are to "honor everyone" (2:17).

In 3:13–17, the author teaches the readers that it is a blessing to suffer (that is, they will receive a blessing from God for their suffering) for being righteous instead of for doing evil.[46] Given this claim, the writer reminds the readers that they should not fear those who can cause them harm (v. 14), implying instead that they should fear only God (see 1:17; 2:17; 3:2).[47] The double foundation for the exhortation in verses 15b-16 is that (1) they do not need to fear those outside the church who can and do cause Christians harm and (2) they are to sanctify Christ in their hearts (v. 15a).

This is a classic text used in support of apologetic endeavors. A few comments will demonstrate why we find it fitting for our understanding of postapologetics. The text reads,

> Always be ready to make your defense (*apologian*)
>> to anyone who asks (*aitounti*) from you an accounting (*logon*)
>> for the hope that is among you;
> yet do it with gentleness and fear. (1 Pet 3:15b-16a)[48]

The first line in the sentence instructs the ancient readers to be ready to offer an *apologia*. This is a legal term for offering a defense in a judicial hearing, but it is also a rhetorical term for a less formal occasion in which one explains her or his position over other positions. In the second line *apologia* becomes *logos* (the use of terms sharing a common root is likely intentional for rhetorical effect). Again, such an accounting (*logos*) could

---

46. The theme of such righteous suffering runs throughout the letter; see 1:6-7; 2:12, 19-20; 4:1-2, 14-16. The writer has in mind suffering specifically because of the community's witness to the gospel and not suffering in general.

47. The text reads literally, "Do not fear their fear," (authors' translation) but Lewis R. Donelson, *I & II Peter and Jude: A Commentary,* The New Testament (Louisville: Westminster John Knox, 2010), argues on both grammatical terms and the text's dependence on Isa 8:12-13 that a better translation is "Do not fear them at all"; see also Karne H. Jobes, *1 Peter,* Baker Exegetical Commentary on the New Testament (Grand Rapids: Baker Academic, 2005), 229.

48. This translation changes a few elements of the NRSV, which reads, "Always be ready to make your defense to anyone who demands from you an accounting for the hope that is in you; yet do it with gentleness and reverence." Also, note that it is possible to view verse 15 as ending a sentence and verse 16 starting a new one, but in this case we have followed the NRSV.

be language drawn from juridical life, but the context makes clear that the author is concerned with more informal contexts.[49]

The NRSV translates *aitounti* in the second line of verse 15b as "demand," which sounds like a judicial process. The better translation is simply "ask." The author has just claimed that the reader has no reason to fear those who might harm them, implying the outsiders have no real power over the readers, including the power to "demand" something of them. Instead, the setting seems to suggest that those who see Christians willing to suffer when Christians have done nothing to deserve it would potentially inquire as to why the Christians are willing to behave in such a paradoxical manner. Indeed, the instruction that Christians *always* be ready to make a defense to *anyone* implies that a defense ought to be offered eagerly, not simply when demanded.[50] As Paul J. Achtemeier notes,

> This command to be ready with an account of one's Christian life for anyone who might ask at any time is counter to the attitude held by many esoteric groups in the Greco-Roman world at that time, for whom such divulgence would have been tantamount to betrayal of the community and their god(s). . . . Cultural isolation is not to be the route taken by the Christian community.[51]

In the third line of verse 15b above, the author names the content of the apology to be offered: hope. In modernity, the church thought of apologetics as sharing a rational argument for Christian doctrine. This text, though, is less concerned with logical presentations of theological dogma and more with the sharing of existentially-defining salvific and eschatological hope. In sharing doctrine, one tries to make a persuasive

---

49. J. Ramsey Michaels, *1 Peter*, Word Biblical Commentary 49 (Waco: Word, 1988), writes, "The phrase *aitein logon*, though appropriate in the context of a judicial hearing, is not itself a technical legal expression" (188).

50. As argued by David L. Bartlett, "The First Letter of Peter," *The New Interpreter's Bible*, vol. 12 (Nashville: Abingdon Press, 1998), 291.

51. Paul J. Achtemeier, *1 Peter*, Hermeneia (Minneapolis: Fortress, 1996), 234.

argument so that the listener might come to agree. In sharing hope, one offers an invitation so that the other might, likewise, become hopeful.

The NRSV translates the hope as that which is "in you" (for *en humin*). The plural second pronoun indicates, however, a communal possession more than the hope each Christian holds in his or her individual heart, and, thus, a better translation is the hope that is "among you."[52] First Peter implies that when Christians share the hope of the church with the world they are not simply sharing an individualistic interpretation of this hope; instead, they are representing the community in the apology they offer.

How this hope-full apology is to be shared is expressed in verse 16a. The NRSV translates the attributes required as "gentleness (*prautētos*) and reverence (*phobou*)." "Fear" is a better translation for *phobos* in this context, however. Given that this word appeared in different forms twice in verse 14, where the meaning is clearly "fear," it is hard to imagine that just a few lines later, the author would use the same word with such a different nuance of meaning. And given what was said above about verse 14—that Christians are to fear God only—the author surely is not advising here that the Christian should fear the person asking for an explanation. Since none are to be feared but God, the exhortation here is that the defense be offered with fear of God.[53]

The "gentleness," however, does seem to be oriented toward the person asking for an explanation. Instead of lashing out in defense in light of the suffering experienced by the church, 1 Peter instructs readers to have the same spirit in dealing with a questioner that a Christian wife should have (3:4). In fact, 1 Peter, in other places, calls for those in the church to be *tapeinos* (humble) toward one another (3:8; 5:5-6 [three times]). Since *tapeinos* and *prautētos* are in the same field of meaning,

---

52. See Achtemeier, *1 Peter*, 233; Jobes, *1 Peter*, 230; Michaels, *1 Peter*, 189.

53. With Achtemeier, *1 Peter*, 234, and M. Eugene Boring, *1 Peter*, Abingdon New Testament Commentaries (Nashville: Abingdon Press, 1999), 132; contra Jobes, *1 Peter*, 231.

commentators see a connection between verse 16a and these other instructions.[54] In the community of faith, Christians are to show sympathy and humility toward one another (3:8). Here, 1 Peter extends that ethic to outsiders who inquire about the church's "hope," even when the person inquiring might be one of the very ones persecuting the church.

First Peter's basic orientation fits with the postapologetic approach we wish to propose. While the church, at least in the North American context, does not face political persecution, it has become, to some extent, ostracized by many elements of the wider culture(s) in ways analogous to the situation faced by the original readers of 1 Peter. Many people see the church as less and less relevant to the meaning making that happens in a postmodern world. The church needs to find a postapologetic posture from which to engage the world (and its own members who are in both the world and the church, after all) in a manner that holds in tension 1 Peter's call to be a distinct, holy community in the world while sharing our hope with the world in sympathy and gentleness.

Taking these things into account, we define postapologetics in the following manner:

> *Postapologetics is a theological/homiletical approach that brings Christian faith and postmodern pluralism into reciprocal conversation in order that both might be commended to the other and each might critique the other by mutually engaging their categories of and sources for making meaning, practices and experiences, and ethical values.*

The definition unfolds in three moves—the content, purpose, and methodological focus of the approach.

## *The What (Content)*

*Postapologetics is a theological/homiletical approach.* It is both a key element of a particular Christian theological worldview and a homiletical

---

54. For example, see Michaels, *1 Peter*, 189; and Bartlett, "The First Letter of Peter," 291.

method. It is a faith stance as well as a practical approach to the church's task of preaching the faith. In other words, the rhetorical approach we propose in the following pages grows out of a theological commitment.

As such, our homiletical concern is both with the individual sermon and with a theology of preaching that informs a cumulative approach to the preacher's vocation. The conversation we propose may not be explicit in each and every sermon, but as a theological stance, it should be obvious when one considers a preacher's week-in and week-out contribution to the church's worship.

That conversation is between *Christian faith and postmodern pluralism*. Note that we explicitly avoid the phrase "*the* Christian faith." It is certainly to be affirmed that there is "one, holy, catholic and apostolic church" and that there is one God, one faith, one baptism. These, however, are theological and not empirical assessments. There are multitudes of manifestations of the one church and diverse expressions of its faith. The different ways that individuals and communities name the gospel could prompt a sociologist to view them as different religions. A postapologist does not attempt to speak for the whole of the church or claim to speak "the only" gospel, but, instead, speaks Christian faith as she or he has come to know, experience, and practice it in particular cultural contexts and through interaction with and formation by particular communities of faith, while attempting to be in dialogue with larger Christian tradition.

Similarly, we can no longer speak of "culture" or "world" as if there were some sort of unity of worldview, values, or communal practices out there against which the church stands. Western culture, through elements of the process often called globalism, is, in reality, a matrix of diverse religiously, politically, economically, geographically, ethnically, sexually, and ideologically distinct yet ever colliding and overlapping cultures and subcultures. Bob Hope is reported to have reminisced that in his vaudeville days of the early twentieth century that he would have to adjust his jokes to fit each new city in which toured; but once radio and television in the mid-1900s became major cultural forces and technologically unified people across the country, the same jokes would play in any region. That element has continued to expand with the evolution of the Internet and the ability to be in communication with people and communities around the world in a heartbeat. On the other hand, here in the early twenty-first century, when one surfs the world by means of the Internet, she or he becomes a market of one, with advertisements popping up on screen that have been selected specifically for him or her. We are in an age in which the world is smaller than ever while conversely individualistic in a globalized context. Cultural diversity is an ever expanding universe.

A simple, apologetic understanding of the relation of "church" and "culture" is, therefore, no longer possible. The plurality of both Christian faith and postmodernism means the conversation between the "two" must happen on many different levels, from many different angles, and in many different ways if it is to have any broad effect at all.

At least one element required for such a multifaceted conversation between Christian faith and postmodern pluralism to be effective is that the conversation be *reciprocal*. This is the quality that distinguishes conversation from debate. In contrast to an apologetic approach in which two (or more) sides stand in opposition and the result is that one side wins by either persuading or besting the other side(s), conversation is a collaborative approach in which the different sides work together toward a common understanding, that is, enlarging and potentially changing points of views of all in the dialogue. Common understanding neither erases differences among the conversation participants nor means success is weighed by agreement. Reciprocity is not simply a communication technique but, instead, is a way of being in relationship, an ethic.

Shared understanding in relational terms means that participants in the conversation better understand the position being advocated by others and thereby better understand their own positions. To use Martin Buber's classic language, by seeking common understanding instead of unanimous assent, we value others and their views, experiences, and practices as Thous instead of objectifying them as Its.[55]

Reciprocity in postapologetic conversation, therefore, requires as much of the ear as it does of the mouth. In a debate mode, one listens to the other side to look for chinks in the armor of their argument in order to know how best to strike a blow against them. In dialogue, one listens to the other side to learn what, how, and why others think, feel, and behave as they do in order to be able to contribute to their well-being and to enhance one's own well-being.

For preachers, such a postapologetic reciprocity means relinquishing hierarchical authority to speak "*the* word of God for *the* people of God." We take an egalitarian approach to the proclamation of Christian faith, listening to others before we dare to step into the pulpit to speak in monologue. We listen not just for what our congregation needs, in the sense of performing exegesis on the congregation, but also for what our congregation and the "world" beyond our congregation has to offer our exploration of Christian faith personally and as the one proclaiming gospel on Sunday morning.

This does not mean, from a postapologetic perspective, that there is no authority or privilege associated with the office and task of the preacher. The preacher is usually the only one who speaks a weekly monologue as part of the congregation's ecclesial conversations and conversations with postmodern pluralism. On the basis of his or her ordination or licensing, the preacher represents the theological/denominational tradition to which the congregation belongs. On the basis of his

---

55. Martin Buber, *I and Thou*, trans. Walter Kaufman (New York: Charles Scribner's Sons, 1970).

or her education, the preacher is typically better trained in scripture and tradition than those in the pews. On the other hand, laity will at times have better insights into the theological/denomination heritage, the Bible or church teaching, and history than the preacher. And certainly the preacher has no corner on the market when it comes to experience and reason. If God is omnipresent, then all persons experience the Divine all the time. Reciprocal conversation helps us, all of us, come to a common understanding and, perhaps, a changed understanding of how we and others interpret this "all the time" and Christian faith in light of it.

From this perspective, as amplified below, a part of the call of the preacher is to lead a meaningful conversation in which the congregation searches for an adequate understanding of the meaning of life that takes account of God's presence and purposes.

## *The Why (Purpose)*

In a traditional apologetic approach, the Christian apologist commends Christian faith to others, attempting to persuade them of the plausibility, credibility, and benefits of the church's worldview. This is an element of postapologetics, as well, except that the reciprocal conversation that characterizes this approach has the goal *that both Christian faith and postmodern pluralism might be commended to the other.* It is mutual recommendation instead of flowing in a single direction. The church (or its preacher) both gives and takes in this process. The church offers interpretations of the good news of Jesus Christ as potentially beneficial to postmodern culture and postmodernism offers its pluralistic epistemology and values as potentially beneficial to the church.

Mutual commendation means that both Christian faith and postmodern pluralism *might critique the other,* as well. The postapologetic theological commitment does not simply begin with the recognition that cultural postmodernism is the current state of affairs in some sociological fashion, but with an appreciation of elements of the postmodern turn as a corrective to flaws, excesses, and abuses of modernity and the church's participation in the modernist endeavor.

We reject the absolute level of trust placed in objective human reason by modernism. It was both idolatrous in placing the human mind above all else and oppressive in that those who named the world in a supposedly objective fashion actually named the world in a way that gave them control of it. Perception and knowledge are subjective. Embracing this subjectivity as something to be valued instead of as an obstacle to be overcome leads, then, to valuing the other who has subjective views and experiences that complement and challenge our own, and valuing that our subjective views and experience have a role in complementing and challenging those of others.

Both the deconstructive and pluralistic commitments of postmodernism have much to offer Christian faith and ethics. Deconstruction invites a questioning approach to all "authoritative" expressions as to how they are prescriptive assertions of power and not simply innocent or objective descriptions of how something is. Pluralism invites an appreciation of the myriad ways people and cultures name the world without assuming that either only one is right and the others are wrong or that parts of truth from the various views must be compiled and merged into a single correct view. Conversation, with a place for mutual criticism, is a living interface between deconstruction and appreciation. We can often value the other as other without having to relinquish valuing our own views. In other words, the kind of postmodern perspective we embrace calls for listening to and appreciating the other, but not to the point that we cannot critique an other's views or actions from our own perspective. Whereas postliberalism's perspective sees cultures as distinct, a post-apologetic perspective sees cultures as distinct *and* overlapping, interacting, and evolving. For example, from our perspective we can (and must) condemn female circumcision, but the church must also be open to critique from others concerning our racist, sexist, heterosexist, colonial histories, and continuing practices.

The postapologetic preacher's role in this reciprocal commendation and critique, therefore, is (in part) to help those in worship see where they stand (concerning some particular existential, theological claim that is the focus of the proclamation) in relation to other possibilities. Notice the role is not to prescribe for the listeners *the* Christian stance, but to offer a tentative interpretation of and position on a text, doctrine, ethical issue, or the like in conversation with various other interpretations and positions. Thus, the preacher invites listeners to become active participants in the conversation.

## The How (Method)

As you recall, modernist apologetics of both the evangelical and the liberal type used the categories of knowledge, thinking, and values of the contemporary culture to explain the Christian faith. Postliberalism, on other hand, holds that the church should maintain its categories of knowledge, thinking, and values over against those of contemporary culture. In a sort of *via media*, the postapologetic task of reciprocal commending and critiquing of Christian faith and postmodern pluralism takes place *by engaging the categories of and sources for making meaning of both Christian faith and postmodern pluralism*. Instead of either letting cultures outside the church define the terms of engagement or assume the church is a distinct culture that is diminished by engaging cultures on their own terms, a postapologetic approach claims both the uniqueness of Christian categories of knowledge, thinking, and values and values that Christian individuals and communities can learn from, converse with, and at times be changed by, other cultures' ways of knowing, thinking, and valuing.

This prescriptive claim is based on a descriptive one. Earlier we said that Western culture is, in reality, a matrix of diverse religiously, politically, economically, geographically, ethnically, sexually, and ideologically distinct yet ever colliding and overlapping cultures and subcultures. Similarly, Western individuals and communities (including Western Christians and Christian communities) are products of, and have internalized such, a give-and-take conversation among distinct and sometimes colliding and overlapping cultures. This give-and-take, however, is often unintentional, unbalanced, and uncritical. So moving from descriptive to prescriptive, we propose a theological/homiletical posture that is balanced in that neither postmodern pluralism nor Christian faith dominates the conversation in a way that the other is not given a fair hearing. Moreover, we argue that the reciprocal conversation be critical in a way that avoids a cafeteria-style approach to making meaning based on taste or ease instead of the difficult task of constructing a meaningful and coherent worldview.

Postapologetics intentionally uses the phrase "meaning making" over the apologetic use of "truth." Modernists assumed that truth is absolute, but one often hears a postmodernist say something like, "*A* may be true for you, but *B* is true for me." To be sure, this is a poor use of the word *true*, but it shows that attempts to construct relative meaning for ourselves has replaced the quest to discover universal truths by which to live.

Whereas traditional apologetics argued for the truth of "the" Christian faith in light of modern sensitivities, postapologetics strives to raise for others the possibility that Christian faith might be meaningful for them in a postmodern context. I can share my faith as having ultimate meaning for me (and my brothers and sisters of the faith) with others who do not claim it without declaring it to be absolutely true in a way that places these others in a "less than" category. Conversely, claiming Christian faith as ultimate, but not absolute, gives me space to receive the perspectives of others when they are commended to me and critique aspects of my faith.

In addition to mutual commendation and critique of meaning making, a postapologetic posture toward postmodern pluralism includes commendation and critique of the *practices and experiences* of both. The reciprocal conversation we propose must extend beyond simply the consideration of intellectual concerns to include the rituals, habits, tasks, goals, techniques, art, passions, interests, recreations, entertainment, hobbies, and tools. It must include the patterns of our existence and the psychological interpretations of those patterns. In other words, postapologetics involves engaging not only the head but also the hands and hearts of Christian faith and postmodern pluralism.

Similarly, postapologetics includes the *ethical values* of both Christian faith and postmodernism commending and critiquing each other. Christian faith commends love of neighbor and enemy, and postmodernism commends the ideal of the other. Postmodern plurality critiques the hegemonic posture of Christian beliefs and ethics, and Christian faith critiques the postmodern tolerance of the intolerable.

# Postapologetic Preaching as Conversation

In the previous chapter, we defined postapologetics as a theological/ homiletical approach that brings Christian faith and postmodern pluralism into reciprocal conversation in order that both might be commended to the other and each might critique the other by mutually engaging their categories of and sources for making meaning, for practice and experience, and for ethical values. At the center of this definition is the claim that postapologetic preaching is reciprocal conversation. We introduced this concept when we examined the definition with a wide-angle lens. In this chapter, we use a zoom lens to focus on it more closely. We begin by exploring the qualities of authentic postapologetic conversation broadly as a way to name the qualities of authentic conversational preaching more narrowly. The chapter then concludes with practical suggestions for sermon preparation that will lead to a conversational sermon.

## Qualities of Authentic Conversation

Our world and our lives are filled with more personal communication than ever before. For just one example, consider the smartphone.

On this small device that fits in a pocket, we can make a telephone call with a family member across town, exchange text messages with a colleague across the state, read and make posts in social media with "friends" across the country, e-mail a business contact on another continent, and surf the Internet while responding to comments made by strangers from around the globe. But increased communication does not equate to authentic conversation.

Conversation, in the technical sense in which we use the term in relation to a theological commitment and homiletical approach, is something that is full, rich, and, regretfully, rare. Communication abounds in situations where the communicator's intent is to convey information, to explain, and to instruct; to entertain; to express opinions, emotions, and feelings toward another; to debate and attempt to persuade; to celebrate or disparage something or someone else as well as to confess one's foibles, and to assert oneself in order to establish one's power and influence. While any or all of these may show up during authentic conversation (for good or ill), none of them are expansive enough to name the central purposes and constitutive elements of authentic conversation.

### Purposes of Conversation

The kind of postapologetic conversation between Christian faith and postmodern pluralism we are promoting is focused on a topic that is framed in the form of a question (or questions) to be considered by participants in the conversation. David Tracy describes conversation (as hermeneutics) in the following manner:

> Conversation is . . . a kind of game . . . where we learn to give in to the movement required by questions worth exploring. The movement in conversation is questioning itself. Neither my present opinions on the question nor the text's original response to the question, but the question itself, must control every conversation. A conversation is a rare phenomenon, even for Socrates. It is not a confrontation. It is not a debate.

It is not an exam. It is questioning itself. It is a willingness to follow the question wherever it may go.[1]

Any question "worth exploring" in such a conversational mode in postmodernity has underneath it a core question: How are we (am I) to make meaning of and in relationship to this topic? How are we (am I) going to deal with the questions in a way that constructs meaning for us (me)? The goal, then, is not to debate the topic in such a way that a consensus is formed in which all agree that A is true and B, C, and D are false. Three other goals come to the fore when meaning-making is the core question.

Even though the modernist goal of seeking objective truth is off the table, there is an informational side to any authentic postmodern conversation. The first goal of postapologetic conversation, then, is to *help conversation partners better understand the topic that is subject to being questioned.* Notice we say "better understand" instead of something like "come to a common understanding" of the topic. Recognizing and valuing the role that subjective perspective plays in making meaning implies that all partners in a conversation may disagree not simply on the interpretation of data related to the topic but on the data itself. Ten witnesses of an event are likely to provide ten different sets of data of what happened as well as ten different interpretations of it. Indeed, one of the gifts of the postmodern epistemology is to recognize that it is impossible to separate data from our interpretation of it.

The inability, and the lack of necessity or even desirability, for all participants in a conversation to come to a common understanding does not preclude all of them coming to a better understanding of the topic than they had before the conversation began. Dialogue about a topic can deepen, expand, challenge in some ways, and affirm in others, our

---

1. David Tracy, *Plurality and Ambiguity: Hermeneutics, Religion, Hope* (San Francisco: Harper and Row, 1987), 18.

understanding of the topic and the questions of meaning surrounding it. To aim for this purpose means participants in the conversation must value critical analysis. Just because we dismiss the idea of objective truth to which all must consent does not mean we abandon the idea that some approaches to interpretation and making meaning can be better than others, especially in relation to particular topics. Along with the recognition and value that meaning is perspectival also comes the recognition that the way we (all) make meaning is finite and flawed. As my witness to an event is limited by where I stand in relation to it, so is my perspective limited by my familial, economic, geographical, religious, ethnic, sexual, political, educational, and ideological situatedness.[2] Since the same is true of everyone else in the conversation, we value ways our different situatednesses overlap at times and clash at others. Conversationalists humbly recognize that their own perspectives need to be deepened, expanded, and challenged, even while they boldly strive to deepen, expand, challenge, and affirm the perspectives of their conversation partners.

Moreover, not all perspectives in a conversation are equal in relation to developing better understanding. In different parts of a conversation, different voices may carry more weight. Consider a conversation about biomedical ethics. When discussing, say, end-of-life issues, a medical doctor has more authority to name what a patient dying of lung cancer will experience physically than does a layperson who read about lung cancer on Wikipedia. Or in an interreligious conversation, a Christian's perspective on what all Muslims believe based on what they see regularly in the news should be given less credence than what a practicing Muslim says she believes or what a scholar who studies Islam says about differing beliefs and practices among Muslims.

---

2. On the concept of situatedness, see David Simpson, *Situatedness, or, Why We Keep Saying Where We're Coming From*, Post-Contemporary Interventions (Durham, NC: Duke University Press, 2002); also Ericka Engelstad and Siri Gerrard, eds., *Challenging Situatedness: Gender, Culture and the Production of Knowledges* (Chicago: University of Chicago Press, 2005).

We enter into conversation with others different than us—different in terms of the matrices of situatedness, knowledge, and experience—both to offer our understanding of a topic to others and to hear others' understanding of the topic in order that all in the conversation might understand the topic better by the end of the conversation. If this purpose of increased understanding is not fulfilled, rarely will the other two goals be achievable.

The second purpose of authentic, postapologetic conversation is to *help participants better understand the positions held by others and to appreciate these others in new ways.* We so often stereotype or caricature others' views (even when we have the best of motives) that we cheat ourselves of a fuller knowledge of others' positions, a fuller knowledge of others themselves, and a deeper relationship with them.

This means that asymmetry is a key and valued element of conversation. If the conversation is composed of people all of the same situatedness, there is little room for real conversation. Instead, there will mainly be repetition and rephrasing. Difference in beliefs, knowledge, experience, and backgrounds sparks disagreement. Disagreement, then, is not to be overcome so much as to be understood and appreciated. We open ourselves to what others in their situatedness have to offer that we may not have (yet) thought or experienced in our situatedness.

Terence E. Fretheim expresses this sentiment in theological terms in relation to interreligious engagement when contrasting conversation with attempts to convert:

> Christians may be uncertain how to relate to outsiders. . . . Certainly we embrace such persons in our missional understandings. Yet, it seems, we have not wanted to link God too directly or too positively with such outsiders, lest our missional goal be blunted or, perhaps, lest the advantages of being Christian seem too few. What shall we say about this? God is present and active among outsiders; indeed they are surrounded by experiences of divine graciousness, whether they realize it

or not. Even more, God takes the initiative and communicates with the outsider.[3]

If we affirm that God is omnipresent, then everyone experiences God everywhere all the time. This may not be the language they use to name their experiences, but, given our theological affirmation, we should be open to God's revelation from situatednesses quite foreign to us as individuals and as Christian community. To enter into conversation with others and to be willing to hear a word from them is to host angels (that is, "messengers") without knowing it (Heb13:2).

The flip side of the coin of being open to others' positions is the willingness to share our own positions in conversation. We are "other" to others. Thus, at the same time that we listen to others' stories and interpretations and are willing to have them commended to us, we must be willing to share ours and commend them to our conversation partners. We need not shy away from offering Christian faith to others as if to do so is offensive. There is a radical difference between sharing our interpretations and (interpreted) experiences of what we consider to be the good news of Jesus Christ openly but without demanding a certain type of response as the only valid one and either (a) apologetically arguing from our interpretation and experiences that others are wrong, (b) proselytizing with only the intent of converting others to claim Christian faith, or (c) condemning those who do not share our Christian faith to some lower status (even to the point of eternal damnation).

Progressive Christians can reclaim terms like *evangelism*, *witness*, and *testimony* as positive terms appropriate to postmodernism broadly and postapologetic conversation more narrowly. Older forms of evangelism and mission that take a hierarchical view of Christian faith in relation to all other religious and ideological expressions of ultimate concern are

---

3. Terence E. Fretheim, "Conversation or Conversion? Hearing God from the Other," *World & World* 22, no. 3 (2002): 306; the majority of articles in this volume deal with the contrast between conversion and conversation and are valuable reading.

surely to be rejected. But a witness to my/our faith offered in conjunction with a willingness to listen to both what is being commended and critique by others hardly fits old, hegemonic patterns.

In a sense, this second goal of helping conversation partners better understand the positions held by others and appreciate each other, then, has two intended results. The first is that through joint questioning around a focused topic and the open sharing and receiving of each other's knowledge, experiences, and situatedness, we grow in our relationship with others without diminishing their otherness. The second result is that participants in the conversation gain a clearer recognition of the options available to them in relation to the topic being discussed.

The third goal of authentic, postapologetic conversation is to *help participants in the conversation better choose where to stand in relation to the topic.* Conversation is open-ended by nature. Multiple views clashing and coalescing in diverse ways not only proceeds from questioning but leads to more questioning. Consensus is not required for each conversation partner to make a decision about what position to hold in relation to the topic and the point to which the conversation progressed in dealing with the topic.

In other words, whereas apologetics is aimed at conversion to a shared point of view, postapologetic conversation aims at mutual but not necessarily unilateral conversion. In authentic conversation all are changed by the exchange itself (in small and big ways), and all are brought to the point of choosing what to do with the new insights they have gained and the options that have been presented in the conversation. We may more firmly stand where we have always stood, in that new insights gained in the conversation helped confirm our convictions. We may modify our stance in some way, in that the conversation solidified elements of our position while convincingly challenging others. Or we may shift stances altogether, in that the conversation opened for us possibilities of which we were previously ignorant or unconvinced. Each of these outcomes can be considered conversion to lesser or greater degrees because all are changes (even the first represents a change in self-awareness).

For true conversationalists, however, any choice made concerning where to stand at the end of a conversation is a tentative one. We make the best decision we can on the basis of evaluating the data, arguments, and interpretations available to us. But conversations, like conversation partners and the perspectives they share, are finite and flawed. Thus we hold our tentative commitments as strongly as possibly, allowing them to shape our knowledge, experience, situatedness, and actions. Yet we always search for the next conversation that will further deepen and expand our perspective and potentially change our stance, while being willing to serve as a conduit for others to do the same.[4]

## *Ethics of Conversation*

While the above discussion of the purposes of postapologetic conversation has focused on content and the way participants in the conversation approach that content, a common term was used repeatedly that deserves pause: conversation *partner*. Calling those participating in dialogue "partners" signals an intimate relationship that can and should develop among participants in authentic conversation. Nicolas Burbules, a scholar who deals with conversation as a pedagogical approach, writes that

> dialogue is not fundamentally a specific communicative form of question and response, but at heart a kind of *social relation* that engages its participants. A successful dialogue involves a willing partnership and

---

4. Cf. Elizabeth Ingenthron, in "Liberation through Conversation: The Inter-religious Frontier," *Dialogue and Alliance* 19, no. 1 (2005): 26, claims that interreligious conversation can function as liberation in that "liberation theology breaks out of that which we thought was possible yesterday, for today we have learned so much more. But we do not have to tear down our past and start from scratch—to do so would eliminate our origins, our roots, the source of our life. We must be content to be constantly renovating and re-organizing the way we see the world around us, to come to the awareness of just how rapidly we are growing and changing and that our understandings are as temporary as the passing of a moment."

cooperation in the face of likely disagreements, confusions, failures and misunderstandings. Persisting in the process requires a relation of mutual respect, trust, and concern—and part of the dialogical interchange must often relate to the establishment and maintenance of these bonds. The substance of this interpersonal elation is deeper, and more consistent, than any particular communicative form it might take.[5]

In shorter fashion, Mary Elizabeth Moore says that conversation is "living with others."[6] To shift our focus from the content and purposes of conversation to living together in relationship is to turn our attention to ethics. This shift calls us to draw out some specific categories of behaviors implied in the high valuation of reciprocity and asymmetry in conversation. We will name three.[7]

First, in authentic conversation, *all participants should handle data, sources, and so forth related to the topic of focus responsibly. Responsibly* implies an open and honest approach to the subject matter being discussed. We should not misrepresent, make up, or withhold information that does not support our position. To do so is a ploy used in debate to persuade others to accept our position. Conversation is aimed toward everyone having as full an understanding of the topic as possible.

Responsibility in this sense does not imply that it is unethical to have a particular subjective orientation toward information under consideration. The issue is one of intent. We present what we know, while humbly acknowledging what we do not know, and we are willing to change our perspective when new and better information is presented.

---

5. Nicolas Burbules, *Dialogue in Teaching: Theory and Practice* (New York: Teachers College Press, 1993), 19–20; cited in O. Wesley Allen, Jr., *The Homiletic of All Believers* (Louisville: Westminster John Knox, 2005), 25.

6. Mary Elizabeth Moore, "Theological Education by Conversation: Particularity and Pluralism," *Theological Education* 33, no. 1 (1996): 41; the full quote reads, "The central vision offered here is conversation—living with others. The heart of theological education is being with others, which includes living in the presence of God, the communion of saints (past and present, North and South, East and West), the interreligious communion, and the whole of creation. Living with others with fullness and depth requires us to understand, celebrate, witness, and relate. This is all part of conversation."

7. For a description of ethics related specifically to ecclesial conversation, see W. Allen, *The Homiletic of All Believers*, 24–31.

Second, all conversation partners *should exhibit self-awareness and strive for deeper levels of such self-awareness in and through the conversation.* In order to be the best partner we can be in conversation, and to invite full partnership from others, we must be aware of our strengths and weaknesses, subjective perspectives, drives, habits, desires, personalities characteristics, and needs—who we are at our core. Three dimensions of such self-awareness will suffice to illustrate its importance.

(a) In order to converse across our different social locations, we must be aware of those social locations and how they shape us. We bring all kinds of baggage—good and bad—into conversation. When all participants acknowledge ways we have been conditioned to approach the subject matter under consideration, as well as ways we have been conditioned to approach others, the conversation has the opportunity to transcend and transform elements of such social conditioning.

(b) Similarly, when dealing with existential topics, and with others who approach those topics differently from us, it is natural that emotions will play a role. Emotions should not be suppressed, but we do need to be aware of them, as well as the way they shape our participation in the conversation and the way our expression of them affects others.

(c) The flip side of self-awareness is humbly recognizing that our awareness of others is limited by our perspective. We must allow others to name their own identities and positions even as we claim the same authority to name ourselves. This does not mean that we cannot challenge others or that we should not expect others to help us expand our self-awareness by pushing us. But the beginning point is self-representation and an acknowledgement and honoring of that representation by others before questioning proceeds.

A third ethical value in conversation, and one that grows out of the first two, is that all conversation partners *should be honest.* The three purposes of postapologetic conversation cannot be achieved if conversation partners lie or intentionally misrepresent information, themselves, or others in any way.

Usually dishonesty arises in relation to our sense of the need to protect ourselves. Such a need, however, typically disappears in authentic conversation because the goal is not winning an argument but equipping all participants for their own process of making meaning. Indeed, instead of striving for consensus, we value disagreement and conflict in the positions we hold. This invites growth by all involved. We value when someone says no to our proposals; we are willing to reject the proposals of others, but in hearing all sides, we all are better able to say yes to something and to know why we do so.

Such honesty in valued asymmetry means that we can be vulnerable to others and that our conversation partners can be vulnerable to us. There is great risk in authentic conversation—not only risk that our core positions will be challenged and/or changed but that others might use our honest self-revelations against us. It is only natural that we respond to such risk by trying to protect ourselves either by misrepresenting ourselves and our views, or by withholding them. But when we are empowered to be honest by removing the condition that some position must win the argument, there is no need to posture in ways that we perceive as protective.

Indeed, mutual vulnerability in being honest in conversation is rooted in trust—trust that conversation partners have mutual concern for one another. Since we do not lose when others disagree with us, we should be able to trust those we engage postapologetically to desire the best for us as we determine what that best is (i.e., as we construct meaning in relation to the communal questioning in our conversation). And we, in turn, desire the best for them in the same manner.[8]

---

8. Of course, people involved in a discussion do not always participate in trustworthy ways. Such interactions are not true conversation. However, untrustworthy behavior can itself become the occasion to attempt conversation about the untrustworthiness.

## Conversation Facilitator

A final word about the quality of authentic, postapologetic conversation is needed in relation to the role of leadership in the conversation. Formally or informally, someone usually serves as the convener and/or moderator of a conversation. While adhering to the ethical standards named above that are expected of all conversation partners, facilitators have some added ethical responsibilities.

First, facilitators *hold all to the above standards and remind participants of those standards as needed.* Even the best-intended conversation partners can allow an existential and emotionally-laden conversation to devolve into argument, in which they can cross lines from valuing the other to valuing their own position more than respect for others. The facilitator must keep more emotional distance than the rest of those involved in order to help participants be the best conversation partners they can be.

Second, facilitators must *make sure that all voices in the conversation get a fair hearing.* A fair hearing does not mean that all proposals made must receive the same amount of time or sort of assessment. It simply means that everyone has the right not only to state their positions and interpretations, but to have them heard and assessed. The facilitator should guarantee a level of respect in all movements of the conversation so that this can happen.

Third, facilitators should *actively participate in the conversation.* They cannot be so removed from the conversation in monitoring its dynamics that they share their own perspectives and proposals. Indeed, facilitators will often have specialized knowledge and to refuse to share that knowledge is unethical. But this specialized knowledge does not mean that the facilitator should claim authority to have the last word and presume to make meaning for the group as a whole in any manner. Facilitators must be open to changing their stances in the same way as others in the conversation. Even while serving as a leader of the conversation, they must practice full reciprocity and value asymmetry in a way that is existentially relevant to their own lives and worldviews.

Finally, facilitators *should not, in convening the conversation, predetermine where the conversation should end*; that is, facilitators should not prematurely determine what conclusions should be drawn about the topic under investigation. Facilitators keep the conversation partners on focus—staying on the questions related to the topic—but must be open to new insights modifying the direction in which the conversation moves. An adult teacher of a children's science class may use discussion as a pedagogical technique to help the students inductively discover what the teacher already knows about the way gravity works, but postapologetic conversations are not simply a teaching technique. Facilitators monitor the conversation to allow the construction of meaning to take place without determining what meaning is worth making for all involved.

## Qualities of a Conversational Sermon

The previous chapter introduced postapologetics as a broad faith stance and theology of preaching. To turn toward a more focused look at conversational sermons, we began this chapter by looking at the qualities of authentic conversation. We are now ready to draw analogies between that discussion and the individual sermon. How do the qualities of postapologetic conversation translate into a postapologetic, conversational monologue?

### Purposes of Conversational Sermons

We named the core question of authentic conversation as "How are we (am I) to make meaning of and in relationship to this topic?" We

101

can rework this question into a core purpose statement for a sermon that is postapologetic in nature—that is, that strives to bring Christian faith and postmodern pluralism into reciprocal conversation in order that both might be commended to the other and each might critique the other by mutually engaging their categories of and sources for making meaning, practices and experiences, and ethical values—if we view the preacher as a conversation partner for those in the pews. Preachers who desire to foster and fund authentic postapologetic conversation shape their sermons

> *to contribute to postmodern individuals' and communities' approaches to making meaning in a pluralistic setting by offering a tentative interpretation of, experience of, and response to God's character, purposes, and good news.*

The postapologetic sermon *contributes to the meaning-making processes of those in the pews.* It does not define truth that is persuasive and, therefore, must be acknowledged and accepted by all. It does not name what all in the community must find meaningful and must believe and do, or must leave behind when they exit the building after the service. Preachers try instead to offer the sermon as a resource that postmodern hearers use to make meaning of God, the world, and their lives in conversation with the many other resources on which they draw day after day, week after week, year after year.

Serving as a resource instead of trying to name what must be believed in some authoritarian fashion does not mean that postapologetic preachers do not "proclaim" anything, that they just throw out provocative questions that get the congregation's juices flowing, or that they just offer a bulleted list of different possibilities and then sit down leaving the hearers to choose. The postapologetic sermon can and should unapologetically be a thoroughly Christian sermon, setting out particular claims about *God's character, purposes, and good news* through the lens of the Christ event as named and renamed in the church's scriptures, traditions, and practices. Indeed, the preacher can and should *proclaim* such things. Primary differences between apologetic and postapologetic proclamation in this regard is that the apologist typically proclaims a nonnegotiable certainty, whereas postapologists recognize that, while they have confidence in their proclamation, such preaching has a provisional character. The proclamation is the preacher's proposal. While they have confidence, they are open to rethinking. Postmodernity, after all, respects subjectivity and relative perspective. Preaching in the mode of conversationally-informed proclamation commends Christian faith to the hearers and even critiques other perspectives. But it does so humbly, in a tone open to commendation of and critique by other perspectives. The preacher offers the proclamation as of ultimate meaning for her or him without declaring it as absolutely meaningful and binding for all.

The postapologetic sermon takes this sort of stance by *offering a tentative interpretation of, experience of, and response to* God's character, purposes, and good news. The key word here is *tentative*. Fred Craddock has often said that a sermon cannot be called good news if there is no room for the listener to say no to it. Preachers commend something to the congregation; they do not dictate something for them. Their proclamation grows out of their particular situatedness and training. Hopefully, their social location, faith, and vocation lead them to be passionate about the kerygma that they proclaim, but such passion should not give way to an arrogant sense of absolute correctness. Postapologetic preachers proclaim provisionally as they represent Christian faith from the perspective of the congregation's tradition in their own individual voices:

- "This is what I believe the church believes, and that it is worthy of you considering believing."

103

- "This is my studied interpretation of the scriptures, traditions, and practices of the church that I offer to you."

- "This is *an* experience of the gospel I offer you to experience."

- "This is a response to God I value and commend to you. And after worship, I would welcome your reaction, critique, and you counter-commendation."

## *Ethics of a Conversational Sermon*

The humble commendation of a particular perspective of Christian faith in a postapologetic sermon maintains the same sort of ethics needed for authentic conversation. Even though structurally it is a monologue, the sermon is still "at heart a kind of social relation." Preachers must handle data, sources, and so forth related to the focus of the sermon responsibly. Preachers should exhibit self-awareness and strive for deeper self-awareness through the sermon even as they offer hearers the opportunity to become more deeply self-aware. And preachers should be honest, risking vulnerability in speaking as those in the pews risk vulnerability by considering the proposal being offered.

Postapologetic preachers, however, must go a few steps further than group conversation in their ethics in relation to a conversational sermon, because they exert more power in a monologue than in back-and-forth interchanges. The preacher is both the facilitator of the conversation and the only one who speaks in it. This means that the preacher must be especially attentive to valuing reciprocity and asymmetry in and around the monological, conversational sermon.

This means that preachers must view the congregation as a matrix of conversations in which this monologue participates.[9] They must be aware of various ways the particular topic and approach to that topic

---

9. See W. Allen, *The Homiletic of All Believers*, 17–21.

in a specific sermon can and will engage the various conversations taking place in and around the congregation. This awareness grows out of reciprocity that is at the center of the preacher's way of being with the congregation. Since the sermon is a moment of privilege in which the community of faith quiets and allows the one voice of the preacher to speak, preachers must intentionally seek out times in the life of the congregation where they are in listening mode, allowing the perspectives of others to be commended to them and to critique their own. This should not be limited to, but is especially of true of, conversations leading up to and following from the sermon and its tentative proposal concerning Christian faith.

This reciprocal listening is a sign that the preacher values asymmetry in the congregation (and in the world in, and with, which the congregation interacts and makes meaning). But valuing it in terms of our own growth as a postmodern individual, or even in terms of the general shape of a postmodern congregation, is not enough. Preachers must value and represent some degree of asymmetry *in* their sermons. They must find ways to represent a diversity of serious voices found in and around the congregation in their sermons[10] so that hearers can engage a range of perspectives in considering the tentative proposal being offered by the preacher. In doing so, preachers must be careful to represent those voices in ways the others being represented would value, that is, in ways that, best as possible in a monologue, allow the others to name themselves and their positions.

The call to bring other voices into the sermon, however, does not entail that postapologetic preachers should relinquish all authority in the pulpit. To do so would be as unethical as to claim unquestionable authority. Preachers have been ordained or commissioned by denominational judicatories and the congregation to represent their tradition.

---

10. For a model of representation of other voices in a collaborative homiletical model, see John S. McClure, *The Roundtable Pulpit: Where Leadership and Preaching Meet* (Nashville: Abingdon Press, 1995).

They have been trained in and set aside by the church to continue studying the scriptures, traditions, and practices of the church on behalf of the church. Preachers are certainly authorized to offer informed, yet tentative interpretations of these scriptures, traditions, and practices. Indeed, congregations *need* them to do so.

The preacher, however, has no more authority in the arenas of reason or experience than anyone else in worship. There are likely smarter persons in the pews than in the pulpit. There are congregants better trained in science, economics, political theory, sociology, humanities, and arts than the preacher. Similarly, the preacher has no better qualifications in the arena of experience than parishioners. Those in the pews have had different and varied experiences of the world and God-in-the-world than the preacher. They know joy and suffering, guilt and grace in a myriad of ways. They have traveled to places unvisited by the preacher and known a range of people the preacher has never met. The preacher has the authority and ethical responsibility to offer a tentative interpretation of, experience of, and response to God's character, purposes, and good news so that the hearers can bring the homiletical proposal into conversation with their own knowledge and experience as they construct meaning in and of the world.

## A Conversational School

In the previous chapter, we reviewed some theologians and scholars of preaching in the evangelical, liberal, and postliberal neighborhoods who have commuted or migrated toward conversational views that have family similarities to our postapologetic proposal. We now likewise note that the postapologetic homiletical theology in this book is related to and inspired by a range of homiletical literature that is conversational in spirit and approach. To use a term typical of scholarly communities, the conversational neighborhood we describe is a "school of thought," a school of conversational preaching, that is, a group of scholars whose ideas, methods, and values are similar. While previous authors have introduced conversational themes, this book more directly plants a flag in the ground, names conversational preaching as a school of thought, and invites others of similar orientation to gather around.

Newly established neighborhoods mature as residents complete the sidewalks, plant trees and flowers, work together for civic improvements, take steps to enhance safety, and develop local opportunities. Similarly, schools of thought mature as preachers and scholars work together to bring the subject matter into clearer focus, to network in ways that advance the work, to identify questions worth pursing, to name and address weak points, to find fresh and deeper beds of research, to think in community about how to respond to other schools of thought, and to serve as a think tank to generate and consider new possibilities.

Of course, the conversational school of thought is not a static entity, but is by nature an ever-changing community. Interaction with others—including other approaches to preaching—means that those who live or visit in the conversational neighborhood are always in conversation about the conversational approach itself.

Most of the works in the conversational neighborhood are indebted to the heritage of liberal Christianity generally and the New Homiletic specifically. Yet, as in so many endeavors in the pluralistic postmodern world, the conversational school is diverse. Particular scholars give attention to particular themes while other authors focus on other themes. A conversational approach is central to the work of some preachers and scholars but plays a role in others without being the permeating force. A conversational spirit is present in some scholars and preachers even when they may not describe what they do in the language of conversation or apologetics.

We now offer a working bibliography of works that we consider conversational to one degree or another. The scope and length of this book neither allows for either a complete list nor a thorough review of all scholars of preaching whose ideas resonate with the notion of postapologetic preaching as conversation, but we offer the following introductory bibliography in the hope that it will lead the reader into a deeper conversation with various strains of conversational preaching. We have not asked the scholars and preachers whose names appear here whether they would like to identify with a postapologetic approach to preaching. Some might be surprised to find their work located at an address in a postapologetic neighborhood. Indeed, some might have severe reservations about the degree of openness to others we commend in *this book.* However, for reasons summarized in connection with each work below, we believe a postapologetic, conversational spirit is at work in these approaches to preaching.

\* \* \*

Allen, O. Wesley, Jr. *The Homiletic of All Believers: A Conversational Approach.* Louisville: Westminster John Knox, 2005.

> Allen views the congregation as a matrix of conversations and proposes a cumulative homiletical approach through which the preacher's voice engages the conversations as a privileged but nonauthoritarian voice.

Allen, Ronald J. *Interpreting the Gospel: An Introduction to Preaching.* St. Louis: Chalice, 1998.

> This work is the first comprehensive textbook to center in a conversational approach to preaching (esp. 63–96).

———. *Preaching and the Other: Studies of Postmodern Insights.* St. Louis: Chalice, 2009. Reprint: St. Louis: Lucas Park Books, 2014.

This short book explores the implications of key postmodern perspectives on preaching through a conversational lens: the other, deconstruction, transgression, social location, and diversity.

———. "Preaching as Conversation among Proposals." In *Handbook of Process Theology*, edited by Jay McDaniel and Donna Bowman, 78–87. St. Louis: Chalice, 2006.

This essay approaches conversation in preaching specifically through the lens of process thought.

———. "Preaching as Mutual Critical Correlation through Conversation." In *Purposes of Preaching*, edited by Jana Childers, 1–22. St. Louis: Chalice, 2004.

This essay uses David Tracy's language of "mutual critical correlation" to describe a conversational approach to theology and preaching.

Allen, Ronald J., Barbara Shires Blaisdell, and Scott Black Johnston. *Theology for Preaching: Authority, Truth and Knowledge of God in a Postmodern Ethos.* Nashville: Abingdon Press, 1997.

This book is itself a conversation among the three authors on authority, truth, knowledge, God, individuality and community, and modes of discourse in the postmodern ethos.

Allen, Ronald J., John S. McClure, and O. Wesley Allen, Jr., eds. *Under the Oak Tree: The Church as Community of Conversation in a Conflicted and Pluralistic World.* Eugene, OR: Cascade, 2013.

This anthology is a comprehensive ecclesiology from a conversational point of view with each chapter written by a different scholar taking a conversational perspective on a distinct aspect of ecclesial life: the church, the minister, God, preaching, worship, Christian education, evangelism, mission and ecumenism, social witness, and relationship of religions with one another.

Allen, Ronald J., and Clark M. Williamson. *A Credible and Timely Word: Process Theology and Preaching.* St. Louis: Chalice, 1991.

Without extensively using the language of conversation, this volume proposes a conversational relationship between the preacher and the text through the lens of process thought, especially 91–129. The authors articulate criteria of appropriateness, intelligibility, and moral plausibility as elements in the conversation.

———. *The Teaching Minister.* Louisville: Westminster John Knox, 1992.

This collaboration lifts up the teaching role as the defining work of the minister in the sense that the minister-teacher leads the congregation in making mutual critical correlation between the past (especially the Bible and tradition) and today.

Bullock, Jeffery F. *Preaching with a Cupped Ear: Hans Georg Gadamer's Philosophical Hermeneutics as Postmodern Wor(l)d.* New York: Peter Lang, 1999.

The preacher begins with a cupped ear, that is, before and while speaking, the preacher listens to others. Inspired by Gadamer, Bullock sees the sermon as conversation that creates understanding and experience.

Graves, Mike. "Deeply Dialogical: Rethinking the Conversation Called Preaching." *Journal for Preachers* 33 (2009): 24–31.

Graves sketches three ways preachers have understood dialogue: internal (as in inductive preaching), literal (when people talk out loud), and deep (when preacher and people come together around "something that matters"). Graves commends the latter.

Hogan, Lucy Lind. *"Homiletos*: The Never-Ending Holy Conversation."
*Homiletic* 21, no. 2 (1996): 1–10.

The writer calls attention to the multiplicity of voices in the holy
conversation, the fragmentary nature of our perception, and the
struggle of authentic conversation.

Kelcher, Alan. "Conversational Preaching: The First Postmodern Homiletics?" *The Academy of Homiletics: Papers of the Annual Meeting* (2001):
393–401.

This paper offers an exposition of conversational preaching proposed by Lucy Rose and Jeffrey Bullock and evidenced in the
preaching of women in central Missouri (as reported by Elaine
Lawless). It affirms expressions of the conversational movement
while offering some critique.

Kim, Eunjoo Mary. *Preaching in an Age of Globalization*. Louisville: Westminster John Knox, 2010.

Recognizing the globalized environment in which preaching
takes place, Kim calls for "the preacher and her message" to "represent one partner in the dialogue with diverse people, world-
wide, regarding all aspects of their public lives." Through such
dialogue, the preacher seeks transcontextual preaching, that is,
preaching in a local context (congregation) that is informed by
dialogue with others across the globe.

Lorensen, Marlene Ringgard. *Dialogical Preaching: Bakhtin, Otherness and
Homiletics*. Arbeiten zur Pastoraltheologie, Liturgik und Hymnologie.
Bristol, CT: Vandenhoeck and Ruprecht, 2014.

Lorensen draws on Mikhail Bakhtin's theories of dialogism and
carnivalization to examine a range of Danish and North American approaches to preaching (including Fred Craddock, Charles
Campbell, and John McClure, who are discussed in this book).
She is especially concerned with the ways that others, that is the
listeners, coauthor the sermon with the preacher.

Lose, David J. *Confessing Jesus Christ: Preaching in a Postmodern World.* Grand Rapids: Eerdmans, 2003.

Lose proposes a "confessional homiletical." The preacher does not try to prove the plausibility of Christian faith, nor does the preacher simply renarrate the story of scripture. Instead, preachers confess what they believe in the context of a wide-ranging conversation with others, a conversation designed to bring about a "critical fideism," an existential faith that is critically informed.

———. "Preaching as Conversation." In *Under the Oak Tree: The Church as Community of Conversation in a Conflicted and Pluralistic World,* edited by Ronald J. Allen, John S. McClure, and O. Wesley Allen, Jr., 71–92. Eugene, OR: Cascade, 2013.

Lose traces the movement from preaching as provisional monologue to preaching as collaborative sermon and, hence, to the importance of sermonic form evoking conversational give-and-take and to shared authority in the service of the sermon as tentative yet bold interpretation. Lose probes the possibility of actual out loud dialogue in the pulpit while calling for moving to more participatory and formative modes of preaching.

McClure, John S. "Conversation and Proclamation: Resources and Issues." *Homiletic* 22, no. 1 (1997): 1–13.

As foundations for a conversational approach to preaching, McClure discusses unlimited conversation, the interhuman, otherness, feminism, process theology, awareness of social location, cultural anthropology, conversational analysis, and leadership theory. A conversational approach to preaching will be relational, real, perspectival, plural, critical, skilled, anamnestic, eschatological, participative, and eschatological.

———. *Other-wise Preaching: A Postmodern Ethic for Homiletics.* St. Louis: Chalice, 2001.

This book is the magisterial discussion of otherness in the field of preaching. Drawing on the work of Emmanuel Levinas and others, McClure envisions preaching as facilitating a face-to-face with the other, a radical encounter with others in which the totalizing perspectives, individuals, and community are fully deconstructed so they can become open to the infinity of others. Indeed, preaching interrupts individual and community with the presence of the other.

―――. *The Roundtable Pulpit: Where Leadership and Preaching Meet.* Nashville: Abingdon Press, 1995.

McClure invites the preacher to host a round-table conversation with some parishioners as part of a collaborative sermon preparation process. The table has "no privileged voice," and the discussion is "open-ended."

McKenzie, Alyce M. "The Company of Sages: Homiletical Theology as a Sapiential Hermeneutic." In *What Is Homiletical Theology?*, edited by David Schnasa Jacobsen. Eugene, OR: Wipf and Stock, forthcoming.

Over approaches that view preaching as a hierarchical "delivery system" in which the preacher presents eternal truths to the congregation, McKenzie proposes a homiletic modeled on the biblical sages. Such a homiletic is contextual in orientation, acknowledges the limits of personal knowledge, and values group dialogue in making meaning.

Pagitt, Doug. *Preaching in the Inventive Age.* Minneapolis: Sparkhouse Publishing, 2014, originally published as *Preaching Re-Imagined: The Role of the Sermon in Communities of Faith.* Grand Rapids: Zondervan, 2005.

Pagitt commends the sermon as "progressional dialogue" in which actual give-and-take, out loud, between preacher and listeners progresses through all phases of the life of the sermon: in the preparation, in the moment of preaching itself, and in the follow-through for the sermon.

Rose, Lucy Atkinson. "Conversational Preaching: A Proposal." *Journal for Preachers* 19, no. 1 (1995): 26–30.

Rose sees preaching as gathering the community around the word to help refocus and foster the central conversations in the community. This article foreshadows themes in the book below.

———. *Sharing the Word: Preaching in the Roundtable Church.* Louisville: Westminster John Knox, 1997.

In the first full-scale work focused on conversational preaching, Rose envisions preaching as a conversation in which the preacher and congregation mutually explore "the mystery of the Word." In addition, Rose calls attention to voices beyond the congregation, especially voices that have been marginalized. Conversational preaching is nonhierarchical, personal, and inclusive. The sermon is a proposal offered to the community for their "additions, corrections, or counterproposals."

Snider, Phil. *Preaching after God: Derrida, Caputo, and the Language of Postmodern Homiletics.* Eugene, OR: Cascade, 2012.

In dialogue with Derrida, Caputo, Žižek, and others, Snider finds a positive route from deconstruction to the sermon as a homiletic of the event. Conversation with others plays an important part in preacher and congregation making meaning together in interpreting the "in-coming" of God.

Webb, Joseph M. *Preaching and the Challenge of Pluralism.* St. Louis: Chalice Press, 1998.

Webb draws on three axioms from symbolic interactionism to help the preacher navigate the increasing pluralism of the postmodern setting: relativity, universalism (in the sense that all people use symbols), and otherness. Though Webb does not use the language of conversation extensively, he has a conversational process in mind when describing preacher and people discovering gospel when interacting with the Bible and other voices in light of the three axioms.

Chapter 4

# The Conversational
# Sermon as Postapologetics

When moving from one neighborhood to another, people will find a good many things with which they are generally familiar in the new neighborhood. There are people, dwellings, and street signs. To be sure, there are differences—new neighbors, different dwellings, and new street names. People can transfer a good bit of what they knew about being in the old neighborhood to learning how to live in the new neighborhood, but they also need to learn some new things. The outdoor furniture that fit so well under the old oak tree in the yard at the rental house in the old neighborhood works just fine on the roof of the new urban condo. But whereas you could ride your bike leisurely down the middle of the street in the old neighborhood, you need to keep that bike in the painted bike lane in the new area.

Thus far, we have described the postapologetic theological neighborhood in contrast with the evangelical and liberal apologetic neighborhoods and the postliberal nonapologetic one, and have called attention to ways a postapologetic theological orientation comes to expression in a theology of preaching as conversation. We turn our attention now to the practical matter of shaping conversational sermons that involve the kinds of characteristics we named in the last chapter. First, we discuss the task of preparing a conversational sermon and then offer a case study of a sermon exemplifying our postapologetic approach.

## Preparing the Postapologetic Sermon in a Conversational Mode

Preachers do not need to learn a completely new method of sermon preparation to move toward the pulpit in a postapologetic neighborhood, especially since we are not advocating for substituting dialogue sermons for monological preaching so much as assuming a conversational perspective, approach, and tone in the pulpit. Indeed, conversational preachers should always employ the single most important quality of exegesis, theological reflection, hermeneutics, and the shaping of the sermon: *listening*. Moreover, preachers can make use of the technical disciplines of exegesis and theological reflection along with many other aspects of traditional sermon preparation. However, these things now live in the bigger and more diverse conversational neighborhood where they interact with others with the possibility of more life-changing give-and-take.

There are two main differences in preparing to preach in the conversational mode when compared with putting together sermons from a traditional apologetic posture of moving from a Christian "truth" to the world. First, the preacher does not assume that a biblical text (or texts) will control the sermon in the way that the Bible does in much traditional preaching. In traditional sermons that originate from a biblical text, the message centers in the exegesis of the text and in identifying the implications of the text for today. The purpose of the sermon is to help the congregation understand how the biblical passage can help the congregation today. The preacher mainly listens to voices that help explain

116

the text in its context and that help preacher and listeners bring the significance of the text into the contemporary setting. The postapologetic preacher, on the other hand, rejects such a funnel approach in which scripture is *the* authority over the congregation and the world poured out on the congregation. In this theological/homiletical mode, scripture is still granted a high level of respect, and preaching might well still be offering "biblical preaching." After all, scripture like tradition has been passed on through the ages, and the contemporary church would be arrogant to dismiss them as if the communion of saints were not one of our most cherished conversation circles. The respect granted to scripture and tradition, then, is that they are claimed to be primary conversation partners for the contemporary church's process of making meaning as they have been in the past. Postapologetic preachers listen to scripture as a collection of others who worthily commend views, experiences, and behaviors related to God's nature and will to the church and world and rightfully critique elements of values, practices, and ethics the church and the world holds on to at any specific historical period. The respect preachers grant to scripture as a collection of others, however, also means that we are willing to take the role of conversation partner in "speaking" with them. We commend contemporary, culturally-constructed perspectives to faith formed in and by these ancient, culturally-constructed expressions and, on the basis of contemporary ways of making meaning, critique the texts and traditions when called for.

Second, conversational preachers should not only conscientiously listen to more voices than scripture and tradition in preparing a sermon, not only be open to them expanding our interpretation of scripture and tradition, and not only be open to the possibility that those voices might challenge traditional interpretations of the Bible, doctrine, and ethics. We must also be open to these other voices offering viewpoints that are worth considering in the Christian house and calling forth a change in us individually as a Christian, a preacher, and the community as a whole. We listen for what other voices have to commend to us, not just what we can take from them, and reshape to fit our current views and mold into nice, little, homiletical illustrations. While we celebrate and honor the role ancient, inherited texts and doctrines play in the contemporary church's attempts to make meaning of God, world, and self, postapologists do not limit God's good news to the ancient world.

In the language of the first part of this chapter, the preacher brings the qualities of authentic conversation into all phases of the sermon. We look now at how this perspective affects preparation and preaching: finding a focus for the sermonic conversation, interacting with others who are important to the conversation, developing the particular direction of the sermonic conversation, determining a form for the preaching moment, helping the congregation imagine the voices in the conversation, embodying the sermon in a conversational way, and continuing the conversation after the sermon.

## Focusing the Sermonic Conversation

A preacher lives in the midst of multiple conversations. Some take place in an orderly manner, but many overlap, some in messy ways. Other conversations take parallel paths while some conversations conflict. Preachers often find themselves in the middle of several conversations taking place at the same time. Preachers are sometimes on the edge of conversations that slowly (or suddenly) become a bigger part of their consciousness while conversations that were once consuming claim less and less of the preacher's attention until they disappear. Most of the time, the preacher will pick up on a conversation that is already underway in the congregation or the culture, but sometimes preachers need to initiate conversations. Out of the swirl of conversations, a preacher must select a particular conversation—or intersection of conversations—to pursue for a particular sermon.[1] Unfortunately, there is no magic formula for choosing a point of origin for sermon preparation.

For the preacher who does not follow the Christian year and the lectionary every week, the following question often facilitates the way forward: in the midst of the different possibilities for the direction of the sermon, which conversation(s) seem especially promising at the present moment for helping the congregation make meaning of God's presence and purposes? The preacher can then identify important voices in the congregation, listen carefully to them, and begin to think about how to involve the congregation in the conversation.

Many preachers, especially in congregations that follow the Christian year and the lectionary, assume that the sermon will originate in the exposition of a biblical text, perhaps under the aegis of the theological themes of a particular season, such as Advent or Lent. The preacher wants to bring the text into dialogue with a conversation that is important to the congregation. Yet, this situation is delicate. On the one hand, preachers should honor the otherness of the text. On the other hand, fueled by the desire to bring a particular conversation into the sermon, preachers may be tempted to bring the text to a conversation in which the text does not really belong. Or worse, the pastor may use the text to represent a certain theological viewpoint when the text does not fully do so. In this vein many preachers read a biblical text as if the text is an expression of the preacher's own theology. The preacher essentially remakes the text in her or his image.

In the case of sermon preparation that begins with an assigned text, the preacher may need to engage the text exegetically and theologically before determining the particular conversations take place in the congregation and the world with which the sermon will interact. The preacher

---

1. While preachers choose the focus for the sermon each week, Wes points out that congregations can grow in theological acumen and discipleship if the preacher gives attention to emphases that appear in preaching over the long term. This longitudinal approach is discussed in his *Preaching and Reading the Lectionary: A Three Dimensional Approach* (St. Louis: Chalice, 2007).

can then consider how the text relates to various conversations in the community. Preachers in all theological neighborhoods experience the phenomenon of beginning sermon preparation with a sense of where the sermon will go, but, along the way, find that the sermon takes on a life of its own. It develops in directions the preacher never anticipated. This phenomenon intensifies for the postapologetic preacher as voices in the conversation sometimes press preacher and congregation toward unforeseen possibilities. One of our students, using an unfortunate but vivid figure of speech, calls attention to the most dramatic of such moments. "Sometimes it's like a person pulls the handle on an idea that has the force of a hand grenade. You toss it into the conversation, and it explodes, and leaves everything you had been thinking in shambles. You have to figure out what to do next."

Toward the preceding ends, it is important for the preacher to pause from time to time, while the preparatory conversation is taking place, to step outside the immediate engagement and to reflect critically on the emerging process. Is the preacher listening not only to enough voices but also to the crucial ones? Is the preacher giving a fair hearing to all participants?

## *Interacting with Others Who Are Important to the Conversation*

After determining a focus for the preaching conversation for a particular week, the preacher needs to identify the voices that are most important to the conversation. The preacher then listens to these voices and brings them into conversation with one another in order to articulate an interpretation of God's presence and purposes that is as clear as present perspectives allow.

Preachers are trained in exegesis to approach a biblical text so as to honor the otherness of the text.[2] The heart of exegesis, of course,

---

2. Consistent with postmodern diversity, there is no single approach to exegesis today, but many

is listening to the text from the standpoint of the exegetical perspective by which the preacher approaches the text. The preacher wants to know, "From the standpoint of the exegetical method(s) at work in this sermon, how might this ancient text contribute to listeners' attempts to make meaning of God, world, and self?"[3] Insofar as possible, pastor and people seek to hear the biblical material more in its own voice and less in the voice in which pastor and people wish the text would speak. The preacher and congregation want to enter into conversation with the biblical perspective in its otherness.[4]

The preacher can bring the skills of disciplined listening, represented in exegesis, to other voices in the conversation.[5] Just as the preacher aims to hear what a biblical text invited listeners to believe and do, so the preacher needs to ask what other people in the conversation believe and do. Preachers may need to engage in exegesis of other voices in the

different approaches based on many different starting points. Exegetical households range from traditional historical criticism and literary criticism through such approaches as feminist criticism, cultural criticism, postcolonial criticism, and empire/imperial criticism. In each case, the exegete attempts to identify the otherness of the text from the point of view of the exegetical perspective through which the preacher is listening to the text. For overviews of many contemporary exegetical methods: Steven L. McKenzie and Stephen R. Haynes, *To Each Its Own Meaning: An Introduction to Biblical Criticisms and Their Application,* rev. ed. (Louisville: Westminster John Knox, 1999); A. K. M. Adam, *Handbook of Postmodern Biblical Interpretation* (St. Louis: Chalice, 2000); John H. Hayes and Carl R. Holliday, *Biblical Exegesis: A Beginner's Handbook,* 3rd ed. (Louisville: Westminster John Knox, 2007); Michael J. Gorman, *Elements of Biblical Exegesis,* rev. ed. (Grand Rapids: Baker Academic, 2010); Joel B. Green, ed., *Hearing the New Testament: Strategies for Interpretation,* 2nd ed. (Grand Rapids: William B. Eerdmans, 2010); Richard N. Soulen and R. Kendall Soulen, *Handbook of Biblical Criticism,* 4th ed. (Louisville: Westminster John Knox, 2011); O. Wesley Allen, Jr., *Reading the Synoptic Gospels: Basic Methods for Interpreting Matthew, Mark and Luke,* rev. ed. (St. Louis: Chalice, 2013). An older work specifically focused on biblical interpretation and preaching, and that offers patterns by which preachers can approach any make homiletical use of any discipline of exegesis: Ronald J. Allen, *Contemporary Biblical Interpretation for Preaching* (Valley Forge: Judson Press, 1984).

3. While different exegetical perspectives and methods call the preacher's attention to different and multiple aspects of biblical texts, preachers should take care to adopt viewpoints that are plausible from the standpoint of what might have been possible in the cultures of antiquity. The multiplication of methods of biblical interpretation does not mean that "anything goes" and that the preacher can just act as if a text meant and means whatever the preacher wants. The preacher's reading must still be consistent with the preacher's exegetical methods and with how those methods would interpret the text in its contexts.

4. The Bible, of course, is theologically diverse. In some conversations, preacher and congregation may need to identify and listen to differing biblical perspectives.

5. In addition to the exegetical guides cited in note 2 above, preachers may find value in broader discussions of listening such as Emma J. Justes, *Hearing Beyond the Words: How to Become a Listening Pastor* (Nashville: Abingdon Press, 2006).

conversation in the same way that preachers do exegesis on texts, that is, paying attention to the backgrounds, motivations, and intentions of the voice. The preacher essentially asks, "How do you—person, text, group, movement, event— contribute to our listeners' attempts to make meaning of God, world, and self?"

Just as there is no magic formula for identifying the focus of a sermon for a particular week, there is no single list of voices a preacher and congregation should consult in the conversations that evolve from week to week. To be sure, the conversation will almost always include voices from the Christian tradition. Among these voices are the following:

- The Bible (e.g., a text, a book, an author, a school of thought, a theme)

- Elements of Christian doctrine (e.g., a statement from a creed, a formal or informal theological formulation of the church)

- Figures, movements, themes, or events from Christian tradition from the time of the Bible into the present

- Contemporary theologians, ethicists, and other theological resources

- Members and groups in the congregation

- People and perspectives in the denomination or movement of which the congregation is part

- The wider church

As we have repeatedly pointed out, the voices in the conversation should nearly always range beyond the Bible. Person-to-person conversations are often potent occasions for getting more factual information as well as more intuitive feel for the other. Preacher and congregation can often pick up transverbal clues from such encounters. Where face-to-face encounters are not possible, the preacher can still try to listen both for the surface meaning and for the wider and deeper associations and motivations in the world of the other. Insofar as possible, a preacher wants to know not only *what* others think and *how* they behave, but also *why* they do so, such as

- individuals and groups who have direct experience with the subject of the conversation;

- individuals and groups who may not have direct experience of the subject but who have opinions about it;

- movies, novels, short stories, and other narrative;

- psychological insights and perspectives;

- sociological insights and perspectives;

- philosophical issues and points of view;

- the arts;

- physical sciences.

Real conversations often bring together people with different opinions. A conversational preacher typically seeks to identify different points of view, to bring them into sermon preparation, and perhaps to invite them into the sermon itself. Considering other points of view can help minister and congregation better understand *why* people hold such different points of view.

The preacher's listening is not limited to conscious sermon preparation. Like many other people, preachers are in constant conversation with the world around them from the time they awake to the time they fall asleep. Conversational preachers make meaning for their larger lives through encounter with the wide and deep range of voices in the world in their day-to-day interfacing with family and friends, coworkers, people, and groups they encounter in the community, the news, the personal events of the day (such as visits to the hospital and the food bank), social movements, and the arts. Preachers should be attuned to the voices of others they encounter throughout everyday life. In the process of living and listening, the preacher can notice voices that can then later become a part of sermon preparation.

Preachers may find it helpful to think about how much time they give to listening to different voices as part of sermon preparation. Traditional preachers are accustomed to spending much (most?) of their time listening to the Bible and to voices that help build a bridge from the world of the Bible to the world of today. While conversational preachers need to listen carefully to the Bible, they also need conscientiously to listen to a wide range of voices. Because preachers are so familiar with the Bible and interpretive helps for the Bible are so abundant, conversational preachers may spend a disproportionately large amount of time with the Bible and not enough time listening to voices beyond the Bible. Preachers need to develop disciplines in which they give significant amounts of time as part of sermon preparation to engaging contemporary others alongside of scripture on behalf of the congregation.

## *Developing the Direction of the Sermonic Conversation*

After the preacher has determined the general focus and identified and consulted the resources necessary to move forward with the sermon, the preacher needs to develop the specific direction of the sermonic conversation. The conversational preacher has two general options for developing the direction of the sermon. Continuing the neighborhood analogy, the preacher might think of two kinds of presentations at a meeting of the neighborhood association—a panel discussion that is a whole conversation in and of itself and a talk by an informed citizen that contributes to an ongoing, long-term conversation in the association. We initially present these two approaches as points at either end of a spectrum of development in which the preacher combines elements of these two approaches in different degrees.

In the extreme case of the panel discussion as a model for developing the direction of the sermon, the preacher represents different viewpoints in regard to the focal issue and leaves members of the congregation to make their own meaning.[6] While the minister does all the talking, the sermon sets out different points of view similarly to the way panel members with different perspectives set out their distinctive ideas. The preacher would critically engage the different perspectives and call attention to strengths and weaknesses of each. The preacher could help the different viewpoints engage one another in a way reminiscent of how panel members engage one another—with such things as questions, expansions, clarifications, and criticisms.

Preachers do need to remember an important difference between preaching a monologue in the analogy of a panel discussion and an actual panel discussion involving several voices. Live panelists can name themselves and present their viewpoints in their own accents. When representing the voices of panelists not sitting in the chancel, the preacher cannot represent others in pure, objective ways. Preachers always portray others, to some degree, through the lens of the preacher's own perspectives. Preachers may need to alert the congregation to this possibility.

At the other end of the spectrum, the preacher could articulate a specific perspective on the issue in the manner of a resident in the

---

6. We are proposing the panel discussion as an analogy for the content included in the sermon more than using the panel discussion as a model for the structure of the sermon—a sermon in which the preacher represents viewpoints in the neat and sequential way that often occurs during panel presentations. Nevertheless, the panel discussion could provide a model for sermon structure. (See next page.)

neighborhood advocating for a position she or he would propose for the neighborhood association to adopt. The preacher seeks to contribute to the congregation's larger conversation about the focal issue which the sermon explores. For this type of sermon to be conversational, the preacher must be intentional about facilitating the conversation outside of worship, modeling a posture of public listening. Then in the monologue of the sermon, she or he can commend a particular position in respectful dialogue with other possibilities. The purpose of the sermon is to bring the preacher's point of view into the community's larger consideration of the issue. This sermon seeks to provoke the congregation to take seriously the point of view in the sermon among a range of possible points of view. While the sermon rises out of the conversation in the context of the community, the sermon becomes a voice in the dialogue.

The preacher decides on the emphasis and approach in a particular conversational sermon based on how the sermon can best fit into the congregation's conversation about that subject. In connection with one issue, a congregation might benefit more from a more general consideration of issues involved whereas, in connection with a different issue, the congregation would be better served by the preacher articulating a particular perspective.

These two elements are not mutually exclusive. Preachers can combine elements of both in one sermon: a single sermon can articulate a range of important ideas in the conversation while commending a particular perspective. Indeed, the preacher may argue for a viewpoint, but in a way that is in dialogue with other possibilities and respectful of them.

Whether operating in the mode of panel discussion or informed citizen, the postapologetic preacher wants to help the congregation understand the issues at stake and consider the meaning and significance of particular interpretations, actions, and responses. The preacher wants the congregation to be aware of how the various elements in the issue sound to others involved. A conversational sermon helps the congregation identify and consider interpretive options. Without dictating answers, the preacher helps the congregation ask and answer, "Which option(s) make more or less sense? Which one(s) have the greatest opportunity for make meaning?"

Readers may well ask two questions concerning the spectrum of conversational approaches. The first is, "What about prophetic preaching? Does the conversational preacher abandon the prophetic task?"

While some traditional approaches view prophetic preaching as one-way travel from the biblical prophets to congregations today, prophetic rhetoric can also be conversational. At its heart, the aim of prophetic preaching is to help the community name God's covenantal purposes, to reflect on points at which the community is fulfilling those purposes, and to encourage the congregation (and perhaps world) to take action (often repentance) that would bring God's purposes and the faith and behavior of the community into closer alignment.[7] The prophet is a kind of theological and ethical ombudsperson who leads the community to think about its own life from the perspectives of its own core values in dialogue with the core values of others.

A classic mark of prophetic preaching is to help the community recognize the need to alter some aspect of its life, to bring that life into fuller expression of wellbeing for all. Hosea, for instance, urges the community to repent from injustice (Hos 14:1-7). Malachi called the community to the full-bodied practice of worship in the temple (Mal 2:6-12). Deutero-Isaiah called the community to recover their confidence that God would end the exile and return them to their homeland (Isa 40:1-11).

---

7. R. Allen, "The Relationship between the Pastoral and the Prophetic in Preaching," *Encounter* 49 (1988): 173–19, argues that prophetic (corrective) preaching is in the service of the larger pastoral goal of building up the community so that all can experience blessing. Prophetic and pastoral goals are not opposites. The prophetic emphasis is contained within the larger pastoral purpose; similarly, Nora Tubbs Tisdale, *Prophetic Preaching: A Pastoral Approach* (Louisville: Westminster John Knox, 2010).

Conversation can be at the center of this process by helping the community consider how its life and behavior compares with its own core values, as well as how those values are seen by others. How do people interpret the world from different places in the purview of the prophet—people whose situations are closer and farther from the qualities of God's covenantal life. What attitudes and behaviors need to change?

The prophetic preacher seeks for the community to move toward a situation in which all people and all of nature experience well-being.[8] Preaching in the tradition of prophecy typically takes place in one of two ways. For one, the preacher may make an assertion *in the midst of an ongoing conversation* intended to provoke the community to consider its situation. In conversational mode, the assertion is not a flat and unquestionable pronouncement but is open to conversational exploration, consideration, and even reconsideration. For the other, the preacher may need to *initiate* a conversation that the congregation has not engaged. Communities sometimes fail to enter a congregation because it has not come into their consciousness. They are simply unaware. A heterosexual, Eurocentric, middle-class male may simply not notice the oppression of people of color. However, some people and communities actively resist becoming a part of some congregations. A heterosexual, Eurocentric, middle-class male may be aware of the many benefits that come from repressing people of color, and, hence, actively work to promote social superiority.

In our earlier schema of theological neighborhoods, we did not deal with liberation theology for two reasons: (a) it has not been as concerned with the question of whether or how Christian faith should be made reasonable to modern culture in the same manner as evangelical, liberal, and postliberal theologies have been; and (b) it has influenced all three of the modernist neighborhoods. Likewise, it can and should play a sig-

---

8. Marjorie Hewitt Suchocki, *The Fall to Violence: Original Sin in Relational Theology* (New York: Continuum, 1994), 68.

nificant role in shaping conversational, prophetic preaching. Given that in conversation high value is placed on multiple voices speaking in asymmetric fashion for mutual edification, liberation theology's role in lifting up the voice and experience of the marginalized is a powerful conversation partner in helping congregations discern how to make meaning in relation and respond to social justice issues.

A second question that naturally arises in relation to postapologetic sermons and other common purposes of preaching is, "What about urgent situations when the congregation suddenly finds itself in a crisis or other sort of difficult moment and needs comfort, help in interpret God's purposes in relation to the crisis, and direction concerning how to respond to the crisis? In other words, is a conversational sermon helpful when a natural disaster, violence, tragedy or the like strikes the community?"

In such circumstances, postapologetic preachers can often help the congregation recall the outcomes of previous conversations and use the perspectives from the earlier conversations to help interpret and respond to the present situation. For example, over time, responsible pastoral preaching that is conversational in nature (in concert with pastoral care within the wider congregational life) can lead the congregation to interpretations of how God relates to the causes of disaster, how God is present during such times, what the congregation can expect from God, and how the congregation might respond in the name of God. The preacher can bring this recollection into the congregation's immediate conversation about how to make meaning in the face of the immediate situation.

In our own pastoral practice, we have found that it can also be helpful to review options for interpreting the crisis moment. For instance, the community in which Ron is a member of a congregation had a massive flood on a Friday and Saturday. As a response, he shaped and embodied a sermon on Sunday with characteristics of a panel discussion that flowed in the following manner: He named the anxiety and tension of the present situation. Then, raising the question of what could be said about God in this situation, he

- reviewed and critiqued traditional ways of explaining God's relationship to natural disaster;

- proposed his own interpretation of such phenomena (the flood, in particular) from the perspective of process theology, contending that God is present both sharing in the community's suffering and constantly offering possibilities for the way forward.

The existential situation of being flooded helped create a remarkably attentive listening congregation. The congregation's feedback had almost universally positive components. Even those who could not endorse the process perspective said they were grateful that the sermon acknowledged their feelings and were grateful that they had a framework for comparing their own theological perspectives with a variety of points of view.

A minister in the 1960s was in a congregation in Indiana in which the local swimming pool was segregated; African Americans could use the pool only on Tuesday afternoons. The Civil Rights Movement was a central part of the national conversation. However, neither the congregation nor local civic leaders (many of whom were in the congregation) were talking openly about the swimming pool. In a sermon in the mode of informed citizen, the minister initiated a discussion about opening the swimming pool to all people all the time. The conversation immediately burst to the surface. The elders (the leadership body) in the congregation held several meetings around the issue. Members of the congregation who were involved in civic affairs brought the subject into public life through newspaper articles, discussions in service clubs, and eventually in the city council. These conversations were animated, even intense, as is often the case when a sermon brings a sensitive topic into the public eye. After considerable give-and-take, the City Council voted to open the pool to all. However, even in circumstances when a prophetic initiative does not result in immediate change, the initiative often sets in motion conversations that bear fruit long afterward.

A key to maintaining a conversational quality in the sermon, therefore, is to respect the listeners' interpretive freedom. Many modernist pastors consciously or unconsciously seek to put the congregation in a position of thinking that only one response to the sermon is faithful. As one of us heard a preacher recently say, "I preach for a decision. The congregation can only say yes or no." Such preachers attempt to foreclose the congregation's interpretive possibilities. By comparison, the conversational sermon seeks to expand the hearers' awareness of the topic and its various dimensions. Postapologetic preachers do indeed preach for a decision, but they value a wide range of responses from and among the diverse community of listeners: Yes, No, Maybe, Let me think about it, I want to experiment with it . . .

Moreover, the conversational preacher helps the congregation not only describe the point of view of the other (from the point of view of the preacher!), but the preacher also helps the congregation identify and assess what the other gains and loses with that point of view, as well as what the congregation might gain and lose. The community (and its individual members) can then decide those things with which they are willing to believe and to live. What do we find meaningful enough to keep? What does the conversation reveal that we should give up?

## Determining a Form for the Preaching Moment

All preachers must decide *how* to say *what* they want to say, how to unfold the focus they have chosen for the congregation. The preacher seeks a movement and shape for the sermon that has a good likelihood of helping the sermon accomplish the purpose the preacher has in mind for it. Different forms model different ways of making meaning, so post-apologetic preachers who value pluralism will want to use a range of sermonic forms over the course of their preaching week in and week out. To use the same form each week implies a certain type of meaning-making logic is the only appropriate one.

In the last fifty years, the preaching community has generated many new possibilities (and recovered many old ones) for the movement, form, shape, and genre of the sermon. In other words, preachers from the modernist neighborhoods sometimes have inherited a significant number of traditional and contemporary forms that support their apologetic (evangelical and liberal) or unapologetic (postliberal) purposes of preaching.[9]

There is no single form or set of sermonic forms that is specifically conversational in approach. Since conversational preaching is more a spirit of listening to and engaging others than it is a conversational structure, preachers need to use forms that help them lead many different kinds of conversations in the moment of preaching. They need a variety of forms that will allow them to participate in the church's and culture's ongoing conversations in different ways.[10] When considering a possible form during sermon preparation, the preacher needs to ask, "How do I think the congregation will respond to the particular pattern of movement I have in mind for this upcoming sermonic conversation?" If she or

---

9. For surveys of such forms, see O. Wesley Allen, Jr., *Determining the Form: Elements of Preaching* (Minneapolis: Fortress, 2008); Ronald J. Allen, ed., *Patterns of Preaching: A Sermon Sampler* (St. Louis: Chalice, 1998); and Thomas G. Long and Cornelius Plantinga, Jr., eds. *A Chorus of Witnesses: Model Sermons for Today's Preacher* (Grand Rapids: William B. Eerdmans, 1994).

10. See further O. Wesley Allen, Jr., *The Homiletic of All Believers* (Louisville: Westminster John Knox, 2005), 71–74. Preaching textbooks typically observe that sermons move either deductively or inductively. Conversational preaching typically has an inductive character, though often containing deductive elements. In real life, inductive and deductive reasoning form a reasoning circle (though not necessarily circular reasoning) "in which the conclusions reached through inductive reasoning become the starting point for deductive reasoning" (73).

he thinks the form can likely facilitate the congregation participating in the conversation, then the preacher can continue to refine the movement of the sermon. On the other hand, if she or he thinks the movement of the sermon may get in the way of the congregation's willingness to enter the conversation, the preacher should consider alternative ways of shaping the sermon.

New sermonic forms will be suggested by a homiletical approach that values the reciprocity and asymmetry in the process of making meaning. However, postapologetic preachers need not reinvent the homiletical wheel(s) in relation to form for every sermon. More often than not, preachers can adapt older, traditional forms that assume a modernist epistemology to function conversationally in a postmodern congregation. In what follows, we suggest some examples of traditional and innovative forms that have considerable potential for conversational sermons. Some serve the mode of preaching in which the preacher makes a proposal that contributes to ongoing conversations in the congregation, and others fit more with the helping a conversation take place in the sermon itself.[11]

- *Panel discussion.* As noted earlier, a preacher could structure a sermon by naming the issue and resources, and then looking at one interpretive option after another according to some logical sequence, such as the order in which the options appeared in history or different dimensions of the topic.[12]

- *Movement from question to question.* As noted previously, David Tracy argues that conversation is best characterized as a process of questioning focused on a specific topic. A sermon

11. Except as noted, these forms are discussed further in W. Allen, *Determining the Form. Elements of Preaching* (Minneapolis: Fortress, 2008) and R. Allen, *Patterns of Preaching: A Sermon Sampler* (St. Louis: Chalice, 1998).

12. This approach is a spin on the old model of "faceting" put forward by W. E. Sangster, *The Craft of the Sermon* (Philadelphia: Westminster, 1951), 87–92.

can identify the leading questions in the conversation and engage them one after another.[13] This form can be helpful as much in shaping the questions that will guide an ongoing conversation in a congregation as it is can be in proposing answers.

- *Thesis-antithesis-synthesis.* This traditional model, borrowed from philosophy, has an inherently conversational element in beginning with the present state of understanding (thesis) and considering the opposite point of view (antithesis). In the traditional model, synthesis draws abiding elements from thesis and antithesis and finds common ground. However, a broader conversational approach would not be limited to articulating antithesis and arriving at synthesis. A conversational adaptation could begin with the present state of discussion, then look at a variety of other perspectives (antitheses), and finally move toward a perspective the preacher would like to have the congregation consider. It might be a traditional synthesis (drawing on elements from the discussions of thesis and antithesis elements) or it might be a fresh alternative in the spectrum of perspectives arising out of the prior considerations of thetical and antithetical elements.

- *Recreating the process of sermon preparation in the pulpit.* Here, the sermon traces (in shortened form!) how the subject attracted the preacher's attention and the process by which the preacher identified and engaged others. This approach not only introduces the congregation to the particular viewpoints in the conversation but helps the congregation think through them with the preacher.

- *Story-sermon.* Instead of simply using stories as imagery that fills out a sermon, a sermon can be a single, continuous narrative. Good storytelling requires that preachers as narrators maintain a consistent point of view as they work with a setting, plot, and characters. Such an overarching point of view

---

13. R. Allen, *The Teaching Sermon* (Nashville: Abingdon Press, 1995), 103–8.

that brings the narrative through complication to resolution might seem to be inappropriate for conversation, but stories by their very nature are multivalent, inviting multiple interpretations. Moreover, the story can be constructed in such a way that the characters in the story represent a range of voices and perspectives that interact in the manner of authentic conversation.

- *Puritan Plain Style.* The sermonic forms discussed thus far are largely inductive in character, reflecting the fact that conversations typically move inductively. While deductive forms are usually less conversational in and of themselves, the preacher can use them to add a viewpoint into the congregation's broader conversation about a topic. The Puritan Plain Style is such an example. The traditional Puritan Plain Style moves from exegesis to application. The conversational preacher would not simply "apply" the text but would draw out of the text a perspective for the congregation to consider, including possible implications if the congregation applies the conclusion.

Of course, there are as many possibilities for sermon form as there are preachers and sermons and types of conversations. The preacher should choose or develop one that gives the congregation a good chance to participate meaningfully in the conversation.

### Helping the Congregation Imagine the Voices in the Conversation

Textbooks on preaching often urge preachers to include material to make the sermon more interesting and to help congregations get the point. Preachers are encouraged to include things like stories, images, figurative speech, comparisons, background data, summaries of research, quotations, excerpts from literature and the electronic media, and references to things the preacher and congregation have personally witnessed.

Indeed, one of us was recently with a group of clergy at a preaching conference at which a new preacher asked, "Where will I ever get enough stories to keep my sermons going for twenty years?"

Such materials have an important place in conversational preaching but with an adjusted purpose.[14] While they certainly add interest to the sermon, they can also help the congregation develop a complex, nuanced sense of the voices in the congregation. We sometimes say that good stories (and other material) give faces to the others. It is easy for a congregation to keep a question, issue, or possibility at arm's length when such matters are discussed only as ideas or generalities. A congregation is more likely to engage a question, an issue, or a possibility when it has a face, that is, when the congregation can recognize its human dimensions, and can relate, perhaps imaginatively, to people related to the question, issue, or possibility.

As noted earlier, one of the key practices of the postapologetic preacher is to hear the other from the perspective from which the other seeks to be understood. A good story can help the congregation imagine the other from an in-depth perspective and, thus, take steps toward understanding what the world is like for the other, especially what issues are at stake and why they are important. The congregation might then talk about the issue in human terms rather than as an abstract matter. The congregation is in a better position to engage real people in real-life circumstances with real, deeply human, consequences.

Stories can also help congregations imagine what the future might be like. If the conversation comes to one resolution, here is a story of what we might expect. But, if the conversation comes to a different resolution, here is another story of what we might expect. Which future would the congregation prefer?

---

14. For a wider discussion of imagery in conversational preaching, see W. Allen, *The Homiletic of All Believers*, 74–76.

While we have hesitations about the use of the big screen in preaching, ministers who do use such screens could project actual pictures or video clips that widen asymmetry in the worshipping congregation, images of others, and the worlds in which others live that is different than the lives and world of those gathered in the nave. The screen could picture possibilities and consequences of the values and behaviors of others.

## Embodying the Sermon in a Conversational Way

As noted earlier, people sometimes think "conversational preaching" refers to vocal tone, gestures, body movement, and the overall demeanor of the preacher in the pulpit. Instead of ramping up in a stereotypical "pulpit voice," the conversational preacher in this caricature leaves behind the dramatic voice and large gestures, and speaks more quietly in a way similar to the way the preacher speaks when making a pastoral home visit or in a committee meeting.

Of course, as used in this book, "conversational preaching" goes far beyond the preacher's style of embodiment in the pulpit. Nevertheless, matters of embodiment are important in conversational preaching because the sermon does not truly come to life until the preacher embodies it in conversation with the congregation.

Here, as in nearly every other aspect of conversational preaching, one size (approach) does not fit all. Different worship cultures call for different modes of preaching, and even in a particular worship culture, a minister needs to be able to speak in diverse modes fitting for different occasions and different homiletical goals.

The voices and bodies and gestures in give-and-take conversations among people in everyday life have different characteristics according to the nature and purpose of the conversation. Some conversations are calm and informational. Others are quizzical in tone as a group works on an issue. Some conversations become heated. A group of guys who eat breakfast every morning in the local diner are quite different in intonation and behavior than a committee considering a controversial change in a local ordinance. Quite different are the backyard interactions between two neighboring parents over the indignity that one child perpetrated upon the other and the rage of friends over the way police officers continually regard them with suspicion because of their racial identity. The conversation of those who lament that their historic neighborhood is about to be bulldozed to make way for a strip mall may have a different tone than a group of students gathering around a cafeteria table on their first day in college.

In a similar way, preachers need to speak in ways that are appropriate to the tone of the particular sermon-conversation. Some conversations are more calm and analytical. Others are energetic, fast moving, and direct. Still, others are pensive. A preacher typically speaks differently in lamentation and in the effervescence of discovering something new and exciting. Personal and group interactions can become heated. Some sermons may, indeed, call for the kind of "conversational preaching" in the pulpit that we mentioned at the outset of this discussion of embodiment. The underlying point is that from week to week, preachers need to use voice, gestures, and body movement that are consonant with the tone of the conversation.

And similar phenomenon can occur *within* sermons. Conversations often move through several different emotional and intellectual ranges on the way from calling attention to an issue to the various discoveries a group makes about that issue (some discoveries inspiring fear, others quizzicality, still others hope, and even joy). Within sermons, preachers may need to modulate from embodiment appropriate at one moment in the sermon to embodiment appropriate to other moments in the sermon that are quite different.[15]

---

15. For example, Teresa L. Fry Brown, *Delivering the Sermon: Elements of Preaching* (Minneapolis: Fortress, 2008); these observations are confirmed by an empirical study of people who listen to sermons:

## *Making Peace with Finitude*

All preachers, regardless of theological neighborhood, regularly come face to face with finitude: preachers can never do everything we would like to do in connection with a particular sermon. A preacher almost always wants to read another biblical commentary, consult the writings of another theologian, or find another story for the sermon. We often leave good thoughts on the floor of the study because we do not have time to bring them alive in the sermon itself. Even when we are at our best, we can be aware of our limitations. Such awareness can be even more painful when we are less than our best. How often the two authors of this book have come away from sermons thinking about what might have been.

Postapologetic preachers sometimes feel finitude acutely because the range of others with whom the sermon could be in conversation is so large. However, postapologetic perspective can be liberating at this very juncture. The sermon is not an end, a destination, but is more like a street sign. It tells us where we are at a given moment, and has a provisional character. The preacher does not have to say everything. The sermon does not have to be right about everything. The conversation goes on. The preacher continues to be open to others, and, hence, to the possibility of coming to better (if still provisional) understanding.

# Case Study

In chapter 1, we reviewed sermons on the resurrection of Christ from the evangelical, liberal, and postliberal neighborhoods. Our case study, therefore, is a postapologetic sermon preached by Wes based on John 20:19-31, the familiar story of Thomas "doubting" Jesus's resurrection, a reading for the Second Sunday of Easter.

Mary Alice Mulligan, Diane-Turner-Sharazz, Dawn Ottoni Wilhelm, and Ronald J. Allen, *Believing in Preaching: What Listeners Hear in Sermons* (St. Louis: Chalice, 2005), 46–66.

As seminary faculty, Wes and Ron preach mainly as guests in local congregations when the pastor is away. Wes prepared this sermon for a once mid-sized but now smaller historic Protestant congregation in central Kentucky when the minister took the Sunday as vacation to recover from the intensity of Lent, Holy Week, and Easter Sunday. He was asked to preach on the Gospel text for the Second Sunday of Easter.

As a guest preacher, Wes did not have detailed access to the conversations in which the congregation was currently engaged that related to Easter. He took as his conversational starting point the fact that a number of mainstream, popular news magazines that year (like most years) had run stories on the historicity of the resurrection of Jesus. Instead of attempting apologetically to prove the historical reality of the resurrection (evangelical), translate the resurrection in terms of contemporary experience (liberal), or graft the congregation into the story of the resurrection (postliberal), this sermon attempts to remove the stigma around Thomas's "doubt" in a way that opens the door for conversation concerning the importance and implications of a story of Christ's resurrection for contemporary Christian faith.

Every year, the exclamation points associated with alleluias on the first Sunday of the Great Fifty Days are replaced with a question mark on the second Sunday. The day itself calls for a conversational sermon as clearly as any day in the liturgical calendar. In view of the context sketched above, the conversational approach seemed appropriate for the congregation in which Wes preached.

With respect to the form of the sermon, this homily contains elements of the panel discussion while moving toward a perspective on the resurrection by an informed citizen. The sermon moves inductively from questions and issues about the resurrection to the perspective the preacher wants to contribute to the congregation's wider conversation. Wes does not take a wooden approach to the panel by saying, "This is one way of thinking about the resurrection. . . . This is another. . . ." Rather, he weaves interpretive options into the flow of the sermon in association with people he mentions in the sermon and with exegetical and theological issues in connection with the biblical text. He reaches the interpretive perspective he wishes to offer when in latter part of the sermon.

The sermon as it was preached is printed in the left hand column with commentary in italics in the right hand column.

# Sermon

He was thirteen when he "was saved from sin..." but "not really saved." That's the way Langston Hughes, the great African-American poet and author, refers to the night at the big revival where the whole service was focused on bringing children to Jesus.[16] Langston's Auntie Reed and other elders in the church he respected had told him that when you're saved you see a bright light, and something happens to you inside when Jesus comes into your life. So Langston sat down front on the mourner's bench with all of the other children in the church waiting to have just such an experience. The preacher preached about the ninety and nine safe in the fold, but one little lamb was left out in the cold. "Won't you

*The opening story is intended to be a little disorienting to the hearers. It is not usual to begin a sermon with someone who hears a sermon and decides in the end that there was no Jesus. Depending on their own religious experiences, and especially their exposure to the kind of revival he describes, hearers might relate to Hughes or feel challenged by him.*

*A further element of disorientation is that the story seems at first to have nothing to do with Easter or the Gospel lection for the day that was read just prior to the sermon. The second paragraph, however, connects the two. It names explicitly the broad subject of the sermonic conversation—the question of the degree to which everyone needs*

---

16. Langston Hughes, "Salvation," in *The Big Sea: An Autobiography*, 2nd ed. (New York: Hill and Wang, 1993) 18–20 (originally published New York: Alfred A. Knopf, 1940).

come to Jesus, young lambs, won't you come?" he said. Many of the children immediately jumped up and went to the altar right away. But Langston sat there as the choir sang and the women wept and the preacher called. He sat there waiting to see Jesus just as he was told he would.

Slowly, the rest of the children went to the altar one by one until only Langston and one other boy, named Westley, was left on the mourner's bench. Finally, Westley leaned over to Langston and said, "I'm tired of sitting here. Let's go up and be saved." And away he went, leaving Langston there alone waiting to be surrounded by light. Waiting to feel something inside him change: waiting to see Jesus. Everybody in the church was praying for him and him alone. The choir was singing for him alone. The preacher was calling to him alone. And time kept ticking by. It got later and later and everyone kept crying out, "Langston, won't you come?"

Langston looked at Westley who was sitting on the altar rail, while swinging his legs and smiling wide. And Langston began to feel embarrassed and concerned that he was holding everything up so long. So finally he decided he should lie, too, and say that Jesus had come and then get up and be saved. When he did the whole room erupted with delight.

*to have the same experience of Christ in order to be saved. As we noted earlier, David Tracy claims the center of authentic conversation is shared questions worth asking. These two paragraphs intend to focus the conversation on such questions. Like a photographer working with a zoom lens, the preacher focuses our attention to Thomas. The congregation knows that the conversation has to do with the degree to which everyone's experience of Christ must be the same, but listeners do not know how the conversation is going to unfold.*

142

But later that night the only sound he heard was that of his own sobbing because he couldn't bear to tell his aunt that he had lied, that he hadn't seen Jesus, and that now he didn't believe there was a Jesus anymore, since Jesus didn't come to him in the way that everyone said Jesus would.

Why does the church so often demand that everyone's experience of Christ be the same? Is it a form of social control, of keeping people in line? Maybe it's a form of self-validation: we only feel our experience of Christ is authentic if that experience is repeated in the lives of others. Whatever the sociological or psychological factors at work, the figure of Thomas in today's text plays a big role for many folk.

In the Gospel of John, after Jesus had been crucified and the women had reported that Jesus's tomb was empty and that Mary had seen Christ, the disciples were holed up in a locked room out of fear for their own lives. Thomas, however, wasn't there. It's unclear whether he wasn't afraid and was out in public, or was hiding somewhere else, or what. Regardless, he wasn't there when Jesus appeared to the disciples even though the door was locked. [HOLD UP ONE FINGER.] He wasn't there when Jesus said to the disciples, "Peace be with you." [TWO] He wasn't there when Jesus showed the disciples his

*At the end of the sermon's introduction, the preacher poses the question that would focus the homiletical conversation: Why does the church demand everyone to have the same experience of Christ? In a playful manner, the preacher blames Thomas for this demand. The sermon then works through the text in a manner that shows Thomas as desiring the same experience had by the others to believe in the resurrection. Indeed, the preacher reinforces the notion of parallel experience between the other disciples and Thomas by use of the fourfold enumeration in describing both experiences.*

143

wounded hands and the hole in his side. [THREE] He wasn't there when the disciples responded to Jesus's appearance with joy. [FOUR] He wasn't there, so they told him about it.

And what does Thomas say when they tell him? "Unless I see the mark of the nails in his hands and put my finger in the mark of the nails and my hand in his side, I will not believe" (John 20:25). Because of this one little statement, history has been very unkind to Thomas. It changed his last name to *Thomas,* and his first name became *Doubting.* But history is a little off the mark in my opinion. Thomas isn't really doubting the disciples' assertions about Christ like some scientific skeptic debating the details of the creation story in Genesis 1 in light of the Big Bang and evolution. He's saying, "To believe as you believe, I need to have the same experience of the living Jesus you had." Thomas is sitting on the mourner's bench honestly waiting to be surrounded by light, to feel changed inside, to see Jesus just like everyone else said they had.

Of course, you know how Thomas's story continues. Christ does come and Thomas does have an experience of the risen Jesus that almost exactly mirrors that of the other disciples. [ONE] Jesus appears to him behind a locked door. [TWO] Jesus says to him, "Peace be with you." [THREE] Jesus offers

*This exegetical perspective allows the preacher, then, to restate the questions focusing the conversation at the beginning of the sermon in relation to the text. The preacher's questions are not only rhetorical devices—questions intended to help the community transition from one move of the sermon to the next. These questions are real. The congregation needs to deal with them. Hearers who have experienced Christ in traditional ways may feel the preacher puts them on the spot. Those who, similar to Hughes, have not experienced Christ in traditional ways may feel affirmed and have a sense that some of their questions are being named as valid by the preacher.*

him the wounds in his hands and side. [FOUR] And as the disciples expressed joy, Thomas expresses faith, saying, "Lord, I believe."

Thomas required a parallel experience of the risen Christ as a basis for his belief and got what he was looking for. So *he's* the one to blame for the church assuming that everyone should have the same experience of God-in-Christ. But if Thomas got what he required, then why didn't Langston see Jesus? Why don't all those other people looking for ultimate meaning, looking for salvation, looking for love, looking for Life—why don't they see Jesus the way Thomas did?

I was the pastor of small church back in the 80s when I was a student. By small, I mean small: we thought it was glorious day when twenty showed up for worship. So I was constantly trying to get new people to come to church. One such person was this thirty-something woman I'll call Janice. She had come to church as a child but had quit coming as an adult. Her grandmother, who was seventy-eight, played the organ for us. Grandma wasn't the oldest member in my small congregation by far. She was in the middle of the age range.

Anyway, I thought this young woman didn't want to come to worship because everyone there was older and worship seemed old-fashioned. She seemed to like

*This story parallels and reinforces the story by Langston Hughes that opened the sermon, but moves closer to the context of the congregation being addressed. The inclusion of the preacher in the story invites the congregation to identify with him in wondering why the woman does not desire to attend church. This is a real question for a congregation that has been declining in numbers like much of historic Protestantism. This allows the congregation to enter into conversation with (that is, listen to) the young woman as an other who respectfully challenges traditional expectations concerning religious experience. The question focusing the homiletical conversation is now firmly established and hopefully one in which* me well enough, so I invited her to church over and over again, telling her I was trying new things and needed new people to help the church move in new directions.

Being the bright fellow I am, after about the hundredth invitation, I thought, "You know, I should probably ask her why she won't come to church." So I did. And she didn't say anything about the size of the church, or about the church doing things in old-fashioned ways, or about the age of the congregants. She said, "I just don't belong there." And I said, "What do you mean? Everyone's welcome at church." And she said, "No, Jesus may be alive and well, but he never visited me. I never had an experience of Jesus like my grandmother had. She knows why she's there leading music every week. I don't belong there." Why don't all people looking for ultimate meaning, looking for redemption, looking for divine love, looking for Life with a capital *L*—why don't they see Jesus the way Thomas did?

Maybe, instead of presenting parallel experiences of the resurrection as a paradigm for the world, this story in John actually presents identical experiences of Christ as the exception to the rule. That is, it might say this if we're willing to read one more line. If we stop with the list of the four things the disciples and Thomas experience, then

*hearers, from different perspectives, are invested.*

*The sermon shifts from question to proposal. The preacher sets out his own contribution to the congregation clearly, but does so in a way that identifies his view as his own informed opinion and not a perspective that the congregation must embrace. Inviting people to consider his perspective instead of requiring is signaled in phrases such* we're stuck with Thomas's mindset forever.

But Thomas's parallel experience of the risen Christ isn't the end of the story. Thomas's "Lord, I believe," is not the punch line of the story. Jesus delivers the last word. Do you remember what he said at the end? "Have you believed because you have seen me? Blessed are those who have not seen and yet have come to believe" (John 20:29).

When we characterize Thomas as the Doubter, then Jesus sounds like he is making some passive-aggressive dig at Thomas for not believing. But what if Jesus's last word is not wasted on an insult directed at Thomas? What if Jesus says what he really means? What if Jesus isn't putting down Thomas for needing the same experience the other disciples had, but lifting up those who are unable to have that same kind of experience? "Blessed are those who have not seen [like those gathered here] and yet have come to believe."

We shouldn't be surprised that lots of people are unable to experience God in some sort of standardized, calculated way. We shouldn't quickly characterize those who don't have a standard experience of Christ as doubters or unbelievers or sinners. Think about how the different ways people experience the risen Christ in the New Testament.

*as: "In my view . . . Perhaps . . . or maybe even recognize . . ."*

*In his proposal, the preacher helps the congregation think about ways in which interaction with others might enlarge the congregation's experience. While the importance of conversing with others underlies the preceding paragraphs, it becomes explicit: "Maybe instead of dictating . . . we should be asking them how the living Jesus appears to them." The way this language echoes back to the preacher earlier, realizing he should have asked the young woman why she did not come to church instead of simply continuing to invite her, reinforces the encouragement for conversation.*

*When the preacher reaches the climax of this part of the sermon, "Blessed are those who have not seen . . . ," he lets the Beatitude hang in the air, without explanatory comment, so the congregation can consider its implications. People who have had different sorts of religious experiences (traditional and otherwise) can be affirmed by the blessing and are implicitly invited to affirm the experiences of others that differ from their own.*

*The story that follows embodies such an encounter with otherness. At the center of the story is a conversation about resurrection. The list of question and possibilities expressed in that conversation is a panel of perspectives stated in*

Earlier in John, Mary is looking for Jesus and still doesn't recognize him, thinking him instead to be the gardener. In Luke, two disciples on the road to Emmaus don't realize the risen Jesus has been walking with them and teaching them until he departs from them. In Acts, Paul, on the road to Damascus, has a blinding vision, and asks the voice that speaks to him, "Who are you, Lord?" (Acts 9:5). The risen Christ appears. Christ is present, but not always in the most obvious, clear, and predictable fashion.

In my view, we have too long domesticated the experience of God and tried to sell it in nice, neat bottles out of the back of our ecclesial medicine wagons that we can refill and resale to the next person, the next generation. Perhaps we need to rethink the eternal and ultimate implications of the story of the resurrection so that we can find God in a wide variety of experiences that the church doesn't control or define . . . or maybe even recognize. If resurrection doesn't at least tell us that God is bigger than our brains and is able to relate to the world in ways that we can't understand or imagine, then I don't know what it does tell us.

Maybe instead of dictating how the Langstons and Janices out there ought to experience the living Christ, we should be asking them how the risen Christ has ap-

*mini-fashion. Many people in the congregation will recognize opinions they hold, have held, or have heard, and will want to be a part of the conversation brought to life in the story. (Indeed, the various questions and proposals are ones that could be found in the news magazine articles in the previous week.) The main figure of the story, Tom, is initially uninterested in such conversation with others.*

peared to them, empowering them to interpret their lives in light of the resurrection, and learning from them new ways of recognizing the presence of the risen One in the world. "Blessed are those who have not seen and yet have come to believe."

When I was in seminary, there was a group of us, primarily from the same entering class, who ate lunch together in the school cafeteria most days. This ritual meal started early in our first year and continued all three years.

On most days, the small talk at the beginning of the meal gave way to a theological discussion about something in class or chapel from that morning. A bunch of pastor wannabes, we tried to sound as intelligent and pious as possible. But usually our theological dialogue evolved into theological debate. During our second year, we had a class that raised serious historical questions about the Bible. Was the world really created in six days? Did Sarah really give birth at such an old age? Did Elijah really get carried away in a whirlwind and never die? Did Jesus really walk on water? Really feed five thousand people? Really heal a leper?

And yes, we even asked, did Jesus really rise from the grave after having died on the cross? Was the resurrection a literal, physical,

*The preacher describes the effect of Tom's encounter with the other in the context of the airplane crash and the morgue in a direct and empathic way. He honors the fact that Tom could not explain fully the mechanics of how the encounter affected him, even while describing its effect. The preacher is careful not to say too much even while saying what needs to be said. Through the sermon, Tom's experience becomes an other for some in the congregation.*

*The ending of the sermon implies that the conversation is not over. Indeed, for Tom, the conversation has only just begun. He has begun to question whether his previous experience of resurrection still holds water for him and desires conversation to help him figure out where he may yet land. The fact that he makes this shift without denying the importance of resurrection for his faith will prompt many in the congregation to continue the conversation in their own minds and hearts. "Where do we experience the risen Christ in places we do not expect?*

historical event? We argued about which account of the resurrection in the New Testament was most trustworthy: Paul's, Mark's, Matthew's, Luke's, John's. A woman suggested that we should think of the resurrection as a spiritual event instead of a physical one. Her partner said she thought that the disciples had such a powerful experience of Christ being with them after he died that they could only explain it in terms of resurrection. One guy argued the resurrection story is just that: a story—a story to live by. What is the real meaning of resurrection? We were filled with historical questions, literary questions, theological questions, and personal questions that also pushed us to doubt everything we thought we knew before we came to that place.

Well, all of us except for a friend I'll call, well, Tom. Tom wouldn't play the doubting game. After the group talked about resurrection for a few minutes, he would always argue that if the resurrection didn't literally happen, nothing else about Christianity made sense. He couldn't even understand how others would raise such a question. If anything was demanded of Christians, he would say, it's the belief that Jesus Christ was "crucified, dead, and buried and on the third day rose from the dead." Nothing can shut down a conversation as

*Relating to others around the table with Tom, the hearer is invited to ask whether his (and others') experience of resurrection might have meaning for them as well.*

*Indeed, the imagery of eating bread at the table evokes the idea of the Lord's Supper, which was to follow immediately after the sermon. By drawing in what follows the sermon, the preacher invites the congregation to continue the conversation once the monologue stops.*

quickly as slamming a creed down on the table.

When we came back after the summer between our second and third year, we picked up the habit of eating together again immediately. And it didn't take many days before catching up with one another was replaced with talk about topics raised in new classes. And it didn't take much time after that for the conversations to become tinged with differing views about this or that. And it didn't take much time after that for this and that to return to the question of the resurrection. We all seemed to struggle with the same questions and doubts we had before. We were all the same. Except for Tom.

Even though the topic of the resurrection had come up a couple of times, Tom had failed to make his show-stopping proclamation. So finally someone asked him if he was just tired of the subject. He finished a bite of the bread he was chewing and began telling us about the summer experience his ordination committee had required of him—working as a chaplain intern in a hospital. I remember how, the spring before, he had mocked the idea of this kind of pastoral work with words like, "I don't know why I need to spend a summer doing this stuff. I already know how to say, 'What I hear you saying is. . .'"

Well, he explained how each week the chaplain interns shifted duties: they would move from maternity to the ER to ICU, and so on. One week, Tommy was assigned to the morgue. It was the week that an airliner crashed at the city's airport. Hundreds of people died. No survivors. Tom dealt with many of the families who came to identify the bodies of loved ones.

After telling us this, Tom said, "I don't know any more whether I think the resurrection happened exactly as it's described in the Bible. Every easy, straightforward theological answer I owned went down in flames with that plane. But, oddly enough, I do feel that I know now, more than I ever did before, that resurrection is real to me. I experienced the living Christ in the midst of the suffering and sorrow of all those people in ways I can't explain. There was no burning bush. No booming, Charlton Heston voice. No small, still voice on the mountaintop. It's not the way I've ever experienced God before. Others, after the plane crash, simply said that it was proof there was no God. But Christ has never been more real to me or more mysterious to me than Christ is now. I have fewer certainties in my life than I've ever had before, and yet I believe in a way I never did before."

And Tom took another bite of bread and a sip of drink, and so